Tile Floors
—2nd Edition

Dan Ramsey

TAB BOOKS

Blue Ridge Summit, PA

It is not good to have zeal without knowledge,
nor to be hasty and miss the way.

Proverbs 19:2 (NIV)

SECOND EDITION
FIRST PRINTING

© 1991 by **TAB BOOKS**.
TAB BOOKS is a division of McGraw-Hill, Inc.

Library of Congress Cataloging-in-Publication Data

Ramsey, Dan, 1945–
    Tile floors / by Dan Ramsey.—2nd ed.
      p. cm.
    Includes index.
    ISBN 0-8306-7535-3 (hard)   ISBN 0-8306-3535-1 (paper)
    1. Flooring, Tile. I. Title.
    TH8541.R36 1990   90-48858
    698'.9—dc20   CIP

TAB BOOKS offers software for sale. For information and a catalog, please
contact TAB Software Department, Blue Ridge Summit, PA 17294-0850.

Questions regarding the content of this book should be addressed to:

Reader Inquiry Branch
TAB BOOKS
Blue Ridge Summit, PA 17294-0850

Acquisitions Editor: Kimberly Tabor
Book Editor: Barbara B. Minich
Production: Katherine G. Brown
Book Design: Jaclyn J. Boone

Contents

Acknowledgments

*L*ike credits at the beginning of a movie, a book should acknowledge those who have participated in its production. Among those who have helped with this book are: Armstrong World Industries; Azrock Industries, Inc.; Tile Council of America, Inc.; American Olean Tile Company, Inc.; Terra Designs; Winburn Tile Manufacturing Co.; Color Tile, Inc.; Mannington Ceramic Tile (Mid-State); Lone Star Ceramics Co.; U. S. Department of Agriculture, Forest Service and Extension Service; and especially Jim Paterson, manager of the Color Tile store in Portland, Oregon.

A special thanks goes to Heather Ramsey for preparing the artwork and to Heather and Byron Ramsey for typing this second edition.

Introduction

*T*ile floors combine the beauty of ancient and medieval crafts with modern technology. The skills of artisans can be easily duplicated by the do-it-yourselfer with an understanding of tile floors.

Tile Floors—2nd Edition simplifies the installation and maintenance of all types of tiles for both art and function. It will guide you step-by-step through the designing and planning stages of a tile floor project to the gathering of tiles and tools, and the installing of resilient and hard tiles. You'll also find practical information on how to repair and renovate older tile floors and replace damaged tiles, as well as proper maintenance for your tile floors.

Don't let the intricate beauty of tile floors intimidate you. Learn how to select, install, and care for tile floors with this highly illustrated book.

Chapter 1 describes the beauty, function, and installation basics of resilient and hard-tile floors. You'll also learn how to decide whether to tackle the job yourself or hire a contractor. Even if you contract the job, this book will save you money by helping you select the right contractor and the right materials at the lowest costs.

Chapter 2 presents dozens of tile floor ideas and complete information on how to make them work in your home. You'll learn how to plan your tile floor, estimate materials and costs, select and use tools, mortars, adhesives, and grouts. Chapter 3 moves right into the step-by-step procedures for installing resilient tile flooring, both self-adhering and dry-back. Chapter 4 covers the installation of hard-tile flooring: ceramic, ceramic mosaic, quarry, and others. You'll find professional tips on how to work with mastics and grout to ensure that your floor is flawless.

You want your tile floor to last many years. Chapter 5 tells you how to maintain all types of tile flooring. There's a special section on what types of products to use, and not to use, on your tile floor.

If your new or present tile floor needs repair, Chapter 6 offers the solution. From planning the installation through gathering tools and materials to making the actual repair, this chapter offers both instructions and illustrations to make the job easier.

Tile Floors—2nd Edition offers the latest decorating ideas and technology in an easy-to-read book that will save you hundreds of dollars. Best of all, this title can make installing, maintaining and repairing tile floors fun!

Chapter **1**

Basic tile floors

*F*loor coverings can add both beauty and function to your home by complementing or contrasting with your decor. Floor coverings also say something about their owner: I'm going to be here awhile, I'm functional by nature, or I've got children.

The term floor covering is used for all materials that can be put over a subfloor to provide a finished surface upon which people walk, stand, and carry out a variety of activities. Floor coverings get more use than any other surface in the home. The covering is not only the background for the room decor, but it can help insulate the floor, provide cushioning, and absorb sound. Performance is an important consideration in selection, therefore, along with color, pattern, and texture.

Floor coverings can be grouped as hard, resilient, and soft. Each grouping has different performance characteristics, and there are variations within each group.

Hard floors include slate, brick, concrete, ceramic tile, and some materials with plastic coatings. Hard floor coverings don't have any cushioning effect, although some, such as wood, are less hard than others, such as concrete. Hard floors are slippery when wet, and a fall can mean a broken bone. They reflect sounds back into the air. Hard floor coverings are, however, very durable and useful in certain areas of the home.

By contrast, soft coverings such as rugs and carpets provide softness and warmth underfoot, insulate the floor, absorb sound, and are not slippery. These advantages, coupled with the decorative effect, have lead manufacturers to design carpets for the kitchen, bathroom, laundry room, and outside living areas. Man-made fibers and special waterproof backings are combined to construct soft coverings that are easy to keep clean and give satisfactory service.

In between the hard and soft floor coverings are those that are termed resilient. They are more comfortable underfoot than hard floors and vary from a slight resilience to a considerable amount of cushion. Resilient flooring is most popular in areas that need to be kept clean, such as bathrooms and kitchens.

TYPES OF FLOORING

Floor coverings, or flooring, come in two forms: sheets and tiles. A flooring sheet is usually 2 feet or more wide and 4 feet or more long. In the case of sheet carpeting, it may be 8 or 12 feet wide and 20 or more feet long. A sheet of linoleum may be 6 × 12 feet or more.

Smaller units are called tiles. Hard-tile flooring, such as quarry tiles, may be 12 × 12 inches in size or some irregular shape of approximately that size. Asphalt tiles are typically 9 inches square. Ceramic tiles come in 12-inch squares, 6-inch squares, and various odd shapes of these approximate sizes.

This book presents primarily the selection, installation, and maintenance of tile flooring. Some coverage will also be given to sheet flooring to help you choose and install such flooring, as well as make comparisons between types of flooring.

RESILIENT TILE

Let's first look at the easiest and most popular type of tile flooring in use today: resilient tile. Figures 1-1 through 1-19 illustrate the various types and styles of resilient flooring, as well as some decorating ideas.

Asphalt tile is still available, but has been largely replaced by vinyl tile. Asphalt tile is low in price, but is harmed by grease, food splatters, and petroleum-based cleaning solutions and waxes. It may soften and stain, has a grainy surface, and is difficult to maintain. It must be waxed regularly. Make sure the tile you purchase at a Clearance Sale isn't asphalt.

Linoleum is made of a combination of oxidized linseed oil, resins, wood flour, and coloring material pressed into a felt base. The word linoleum should be used only for this product, since it doesn't perform like vinyl floor coverings and requires different care. While linoleum is resistant to grease, it can be harmed by alkalis. Therefore, it cannot be installed on concrete that is in direct contact with the ground because moisture and alkalis can move up through the concrete and into the felt backing and linoleum.

1-1   Vinyl resilient floor tile.

1-2 Resilient floor tile in the kitchen and dining area.

1-3 Vinyl resilient no-wax floor tile in the hallway.

1-4 Vinyl resilient no-wax floor tile that looks like a wood floor.

1-5 Vinyl resilient no-wax floor tile in the living area.

1-6 Vinyl floor tile designed to simulate mosiac tile.

1-7 Vinyl resilient tile looks like it's been freshly waxed.

1-8 Resilient no-wax floor tile can brighten up a kitchen floor.

1-10 Resilient no-wax floor tile simulates ceramic tile in a bathroom.

1-11   This floor design is perfect for an entryway or hallway.

1-12   This resilient no-wax floor tile is designed to look like a parquet wood floor.

1-13 No-wax floor tiles in this 12 × 12-inch design looks like sheet flooring.

1-14 There are numerous unique designs offered in resilient tile flooring.

1-16 Resilient no-wax floor tile with a glazed tile design.

1-17 Simulated old tile design of resilient floor tile.

1-18 Resilient tile can also simulate pavers.

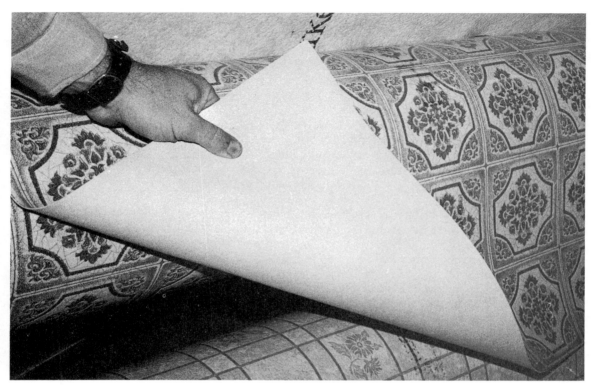

1-19 Resilient vinyl sheet flooring.

Because alkali materials are used in floor washing powders, care must be taken to use mild products. They should be left on the linoleum for only two or three minutes. The surface of linoleum is porous and should be sealed before a wax or liquid floor dressing is applied. Traffic leaves scratches, digs, and scrapes on linoleum so that it may have a worn appearance before its useful life is over. Tips on maintaining linoleum floors will be presented in Chapter 5.

Vinyl tile is composed of vinyl resins and composition fillers. It is moderate in cost, very durable, and easily cleaned. It can be used over on-grade, below-grade, and suspended floors. Resistance to alkali and grease are exceptionally good.

Homogeneous vinyl tile is unbacked and usually has a uniform composition. It is higher in cost than vinyl tile. It can be installed on suspended wood subfloors, or over on-grade or below-grade concrete. It is durable and easily cleaned.

Vinyl sheet flooring is available as inlaid (the pattern goes out throughout the wear layer of vinyl) and as rotogravure (the pattern is printed on a sheet that is then covered with a layer of clear vinyl which is the wearing surface). The thickness of both types of wear layers varies with the price of the floor covering. The range for vinyl sheet coverings range from no cushion at all to a thick cushion beneath the wear layer.

Special backing material is applied to some vinyl coverings so they can be used on concrete that comes in contact with the ground.

No-wax sheet flooring is not a vinyl surface, but a new product to which, it is claimed, wax will not stick. If the gloss dulls after several years of service, the manufacturer can provide a special floor finish for periodic application in traffic areas.

SELECTING RESILIENT TILE

There are a number of important factors to consider before you select a product from the broad group called resilient floor coverings. Look at the gauge or thickness, resilience, under-foot comfort, quietness, light reflectivity, effects of radiant heating, flammability ratings, and relative cost.

The durability of the floor coverings depends partly on the thickness of the wear layer. Modern manufacturing methods and improved materials have resulted in durable wear layers that are thinner than formerly needed. The wear layer is either that part containing the color and pattern or the transparent layer above it. Inlaid vinyl and linoleum have the pattern all the way through the layer. Printed-vinyl sheet floorings and some tiles have a wear layer above the pattern, which varies from 6 mils to several times that thickness. Normally, at least 10 mils is needed to protect the floor covering from damage by sharp objects.

Quietness and comfort vary according to the total thickness of the floor coverings. The thicker floor coverings absorb more impact and are therefore less noisy. At the same time, they provide more cushion for walking and standing. Cushioned floor coverings vary both in thickness and in the amount of cushion provided.

Resilience is the measure of the elasticity of a material, or a material's ability to regain its original shape after being indented. The impact from walking traffic can be several thousand pounds per square inch, especially with tiny heels. It isn't possible to control the indention that flooring may receive, but the results can be minimized if light, multicolored floorings are chosen in patterns that swirl, have marble-like graining, or are terrazzo, mosaic, or spatter-dash mottling. Embossed surface textures and low-gloss finishes also conceal indentions. To reduce the indention from heavy furniture, use floor protectors of adequate size under furniture legs. Don't use dark protectors, though, because they discolor both vinyl and linoleum coverings.

The underfoot comfort of resilient floor coverings is affected by the subfloor material, as well as the composition of the floor covering. On concrete, a cushioned floor covering will help reduce fatigue from walking and standing. The thicker cushions will also provide some insulation from cold floors.

The sound created by the impact of foot traffic is a common source of annoyance. The sound seems to reverberate to adjoining rooms and is pronounced in the room underneath. Most resilient floor coverings produce less noise than hardwood floors, but cushioned floor coverings create much less sound than the uncushioned resilient coverings. This cushion is, however, not enough to stop sounds coming through the floor from the room above.

Room noises, such as voices and equipment sounds, are not absorbed by the resilient floor coverings as they are by the textured surface of carpeting. The smooth surface of resilient coverings allows the sound to reverberate.

The amount of light reflected by the floor covering helps determine how much light is available for seeing. The tints closest to white will reflect the most light, whereas medium and dark colors will absorb a great deal of the daylight or electric light that reaches the floor.

The amount of gloss on the surface of the floor covering has an effect on the appearance of the finished floor. Smooth, shiny flooring materials tend to show up any minor irregularities in the subfloor surfaces and, therefore, require more subfloor preparations and inspections before they are installed. Embossed floor coverings soften the light reflection.

Regarding the effects of radiant heating, tests show that there is almost no loss of heating efficiency when resilient flooring materials are used. No harmful effects on the floor coverings have resulted from their use on radiant heated floors either.

Floor coverings can be tested for flame spread where this is a concern. Currently, a government directive known as the Hill-Burton Regulations is used to test floor coverings for hospital and medical facilities. Information about the rating of a particular floor covering can be obtained from the manufacturer.

RESILIENT FLOORING COSTS

Several factors besides the cost per square foot, should be considered when determining the cost of a floor covering. Perhaps the most important cost is the expense of preparing the subfloor and doing the installation work. The most expensive floor covering may not perform well if the subfloor is not suitable or the adhesive or workmanship is not of good quality. Installers vary in their experience and reliability, as is true with any trade.

Manufacturers of resilient tile and other floor coverings specify the kind of subfloor that is needed for each covering. Retail dealers have this information. Also, Chapter 3 will offer information on subfloor requirements. The method of installation may make it possible for a new resilient covering to be placed over an old covering. The advice of the floor covering retailer can be very helpful.

The size and shape of the room may make tile more economical than sheet flooring because of irregularities in the room that may require much fitting and loss of material. The width of the room may require more yardage in sheet coverings than would be needed in tile.

Do-it-yourself installation saves a great deal of money where it is feasible. Some floor coverings can be cut and laid without adhesive using either double-faced tape or adhesive around the edges. Self-adhesive tiles can be laid by an amateur. Some tiles carry a 5-year guarantee that they

will bond to the subfloor when the manufacturers instructions are followed.

A HISTORY OF TILE

As you can imagine, resilient tile is a fairly new product in the history
of mankind. The earliest tiles used for flooring and walls were hard tiles.
The use of glazed tiles dates from about 4,000 B.C.—two millenniums
before Moses was given stone tablets. Excavations of structures built prior
to this era seems to indicate that the age of tiles stemmed from man's earliest experience with the most primitive plastic—common earth. First, man
learned to mold and sun-dry various types of earth. From there it was a
simple step to discover the advantage of baking with artificial heat. This
led to the discovery that certain materials, if heated sufficiently, would
melt and form a glaze. Impressed with the hardness of this glaze, as well
as the possible decorative effects, builders experimented further. These
experiments eventually resulted in a finished product comparable to that
which we use today.

Some of the more ornate buildings of ancient times had tile work that
was even more elaborate than what we see now. Certain mosaics that
depict the life of bygone civilizations and inscriptions found on tombs
and other structures employed bits of tile-glazed surfaces. Somewhat
later, the Aztecs and Incas produced styles and designs of their own, most
of which were handmade. Even today, Mexican handmade tile is popular
in the United States, particularly in Spanish-style homes and churches.

In modern times, manufacturers have developed better processes
and materials for glazes, bisques, and installation. What may have
required a craftsman in the past, now can be accomplished by a do-it-
yourselfer. Refractories have been improved until a host of materials are
now available. Recently, new kinds of tile were put on the market, including aluminum with a baked-enamel finish, steel, cement with a terra-cotta
surface, and plastic tiles. Wood and fiberboard have likewise been coated
with lacquer or plastic, and are available in large scored sheets. Nearly all
these coverings are installed with a mastic substance as the adhesive
agent. A newer innovation is a substance much like white portland
cement. This is known as the thin-wall method. It will be covered in
Chapter 4.

HARD TILE

There are literally thousands of types and designs of hard tiles available today for installation on floors, walls, and other surfaces. They range
from small ceramic chips to large flat stones. Figures 1-20 through 1-31
illustrate hard tiles and design ideas.

There are two general types of ceramic tiles. Perhaps the best known
are the $4^{1}/_{4} \times 4^{1}/_{4}$-inch tiles that are made in three different textures. The
high-gloss type is designed for use on walls, ceilings, trim work, and
drainboard splashes—in fact everywhere except on floors and steps.

Tile Council of America

1-20 Ceramic mosaic hard tile installed in the kitchen and dining area.

1-21   Ceramic mosaic hard tile installed in the entryway.

1-22. Ceramic mosaic tile used in an Early American dining room.

Glazed tiles, however, are often made in various other sizes. In the case of ceramic tiles, they may be 1-inch hexagons, 3/4-inch squares, or numerous rectangular sizes. High-gloss tiles are rarely used on floors.

Another type of glazed tile, known as crystal glazed, has a rough, granular texture, which is more or less slipproof. Crystal-glazed tiles may be used on floors in any but public buildings, and are one of the most popular tile for use in all situations where a glazed tile is desired. Two intermediate glazes known as matte and satin matte, are also available. They are valuable in that they relieve the glare of high-gloss tiles.

1-23   Quarry tile in the entryway.

1-24   Quarry tile can also add a decorative dimension to the living room.

Tile Council of America

1-25   Ceramic tile can also be used for more contemporary designs.

The simplest types of tiles are those that are made of some kind of clay, which is molded in simple hand molds, and baked. In order to made them more decorative, various colored glazes are applied. The makers of more primitive tiles were content with plain unglazed pieces. A modern tile of this type is the Spanish patio tile. It is made of terra-cotta, and is usually thick and of large size.

I-26 Ceramic tile can beautify floors, walls, and even countertops.

More elaborate types of tile are made in Mexico, where floral patterns in or under the glaze are used. Some ceramic tile must be soaked in water before setting. From thirty minutes to 2 hours may be required for saturation. The bisque, or main body of these tiles, is made of red, cream, or the more common, white clay. White clay of one type is known as China clay and is often used in pottery making.

1-27 Greenhouse additions often use ceramic floor tile.

1-28   Ceramic tile in the great room.

Tile Council of America

1-29 Unglazed ceramic tile.

1-30 Today's ceramic tile comes in an infinite range of sizes, shapes, and colors.

Other ceramic tiles have a silicon base and may incorporate little or no clay, depending on the color desired. These tiles are pressed in hydraulic molds and are either unglazed or glazed. Similar to these, but generally larger, are the quarry tiles that usually have a red dish brick color. Modern methods of manufacturing generally produce the vitreous type or those that require no soaking.

I-3I   Ceramic tile can be used to develop mosaic designs in your floor.

Ceramic tiles are often unglazed, in which case they are suitable for either floors or walls. They are ideal for swimming pools, curved surfaces, or wherever small tile is needed.

Encaustic tiles are made of terra-cotta clays of two or more colors. One color forms the bisque into which designs are etched and the other color is pressed into the depressions that comprise the design. The tile surface is then smoothed, which leaves a sharp contrast of colors.

Sometimes encaustic tiles are glazed, but the majority are unglazed and have a surface much like quarry tile. Glazed encaustic tiles are used as stair risers and on walls.

Quarry tiles are made with a silica base and varying amounts of clay. They are first pressed in a hydraulic press and then baked. Because of the excessive quantity of silica and the density of these tiles, they don't absorb water in any appreciable quantity. The texture of broken pieces shows the vitreous or glassy structure.

Quarry tiles are manufactured in assorted sizes and thicknesses and are either glazed or unglazed. Unglazed types lend themselves to floor work, while the glazed kinds are better suited for walls or other vertical situations.

Patio tiles are similar in appearance to quarry tile but are made of terra-cotta or have a clay base. They are never glazed and must be soaked before setting. They are used for floors and patios. Their large size eliminates their use in small areas.

Pavers are similar to ceramic mosaic tile in composition, but are thicker and larger. They look much like unglazed tile. Like quarry tile and ceramic mosaics, they can be used outdoors.

Hard tiles such as quarry tiles, pavers, and some glazed ceramic tiles are frequently installed under wood stoves. The tiles must have a good subfloor to adhere to and be of a strength and thickness that eliminates the chance of breakage.

SELECTING HARD TILES

The selection and purchase of hard tiles can be a pain or joy, depending on how much you know about them before you step into the first flooring store. I'll cover a number of topics and ideas to help you in this selection. In addition, FIGS. 1-32 through 1-39 illustrate the retail selection process.

First, make sure that the tile you decide upon is suitable for floors. Tiles for floors are generally heavier and thicker than wall tiles, and the finishes are either matte or textured. The very high-gloss glazes would obviously scratch underfoot, so they are best reserved for walls.

Color is a matter of taste, but it's best to choose conservatively. Because a tile floor is likely to be down for the life of the house, it should be so neutral that it would go with the broadest possible range of furnishing styles and colors.

The neutral colors include white, off-white, tan, gray, and brown. These hues are plentiful in glazed floor tiles, as well as in unglazed ceramic mosaics, which are those tiny 1- and 2-inch squares popular in designer homes.

All of the earth tones, which are natural to unglazed quarry tile and pavers, are good neutrals. Until recently, these products came only in terra-cotta. They now run the gamut of earth colors from the palest sand to the darkest umber.

You can use quarry tiles or pavers in any interior except the most formal ones. Pale tiles blend well in contemporary rooms. Warm reddish and brown tones suit colonial and country decors. The darkest colors retain heat extremely well, so they should be used in sun spaces, greenhouses, and other passive solar additions or retrofits.

Choose glazed tiles for formal, traditional rooms. Dark green, burgundy, and gold tones are beautiful choices for interiors that feature fine antiques. Black and white checkerboard designs are classics for French or Italian period rooms.

Precisely cut, smooth tiles look best in contemporary rooms. Tiles with a hand-crafted look, which can be achieved with deliberately uneven edges and random surface textures, are best for traditional and country homes.

Grout, the material that fills the joints between the tile, can help the floor seem more interesting. For graphic impact, choose a grout color that contrasts sharply with the tile. For a monochromatic, quiet effect, choose a grout color that matches the tile.

I-32   Typical retail floor-tile display.

I-33 Watch for special prices on flooring, especially in the fall and spring.

I-34 Tiles come in a variety of sizes and shapes.

1-35 Typical ceramic tiles.

Ceramic mosaics usually come in 1- or 2-inch squares, as well as in small rectangles and hexagon shapes. There are glazed and unglazed ceramic mosaic tiles. Generally, only the unglazed tiles should be used for floors. Ceramic mosaics are usually mounted on 1-square-foot sheets with equal ground spacing for easy installation. If you need just a few tiles cut out of the sheet to create a pattern, merely cut the bonding material with ordinary scissors. Don't forget to include the grout line spaces, however, when you lay out loose tiles.

HARD-TILE GREENHOUSE EFFECT

Few homes use hard tiles throughout the house. Rather, they are used selectively in entryways, halls, kitchens, baths, and in add-on greenhouse rooms. In fact, a greenhouse or sun room is an excellent place for hard tiles that capture and release solar energy.

Greenhouses are no longer just for gardeners. Increasingly, they are added onto houses to cut heating bills and, at the same time, add welcome square footage. According to the Tile Council of America, a greenhouse addition can act as a natural solar collector and provide appreciable heat gains from the Sun. Step-by-step instructions and illustrations for installing such a tile-floored greenhouse are offered in Chapter 4.

1-36 Display of various ceramic-mosaic tile sheets.

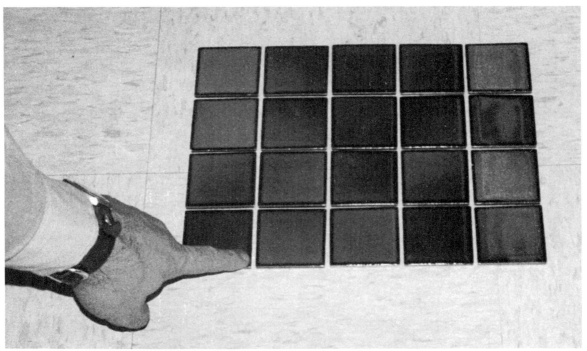

1-37   Sheets of ceramic-mosaic tiles are uniformly spaced for grouting.

1-38   Ceramic tile also comes in sheets with uniform spacing.

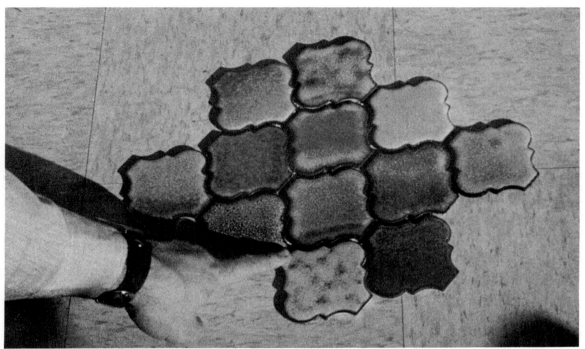

I-40   Ceramic tile can also be purchased in unique shapes.

The key to solar use is the thermal mass of hard tiles that absorbs warmth from the Sun and slowly releases it as the air cools in the evening or on cloudy days. The thermal mass is usually supplied by a thick concrete slab. Ceramic tile is the only floor covering that can be used on top of the slab in such solar installations.

Heavy quarry tiles or pavers are great choices for sunspace floors. Dark colors absorb heat better than light ones, so terra-cottas and browns are the best choices. Unglazed, natural tile has also been found to absorb heat better than the glazed types.

About 4 inches of floor or wall mass are needed for ceramic tile to serve as a heat sink. It's best to ensure that the heat-absorbing surfaces are not covered with rugs, a lot of furniture, paintings, plants, or other decorations. Masonry planters, tiled to match the floor, and tile-topped counters will soak up the Sun's rays, too. Use black water-filled drums as the base for counters or potted tables to increase the room's thermal properties.

Some greenhouse additions harness more Sun than they need. This heat can be used in adjoining rooms. Doors and/or registers can distribute the air. In the summer, awnings or blinds should be used to keep the Sun out of the greenhouse. Such shielded tile floors and walls can also help keep the inside cool during the hot months.

Remember that a greenhouse that is supposed to harness the heat of the Sun must face the quadrant from the southeast to the southwest. Also consider the trees around the house. Deciduous trees that provide summer shade are usually fine, but make sure that their branches aren't so dense that they block out too much Sun in the winter.

Keep in mind, too, that in some cases the addition of a greenhouse to your home will make you eligible for a solar energy tax credit. Discuss the requirements with your tax accountant or the Internal Revenue Service.

Chapter **2**

Planning tile floors

Once you've selected the type of tile floor you will install, you are ready for the most important task—planning. Good planning is important because it helps guarantee a satisfactory floor, minimizes waste, reduces the number of problems, cuts costs, and makes the job enjoyable. Good planning includes understanding the following: the basics of floor construction and covering, how to select and use tiles and tools, how to estimate material requirements, and how to prepare for the job.

RESILIENT FLOOR BASES

Resilient floors should not be installed directly over a board or plank subfloor. An underlayment grade of wood-based panels such as plywood, particleboard, and hardboard is widely used for suspended floor applications (FIG. 2-1).

Plywood or particleboard panels, which are 4 × 8 feet and range in thickness from 3/8 to 3/4 inch, are generally used in new construction.

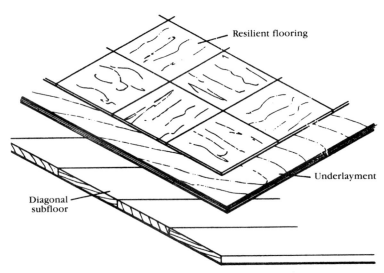

2-1.   Using underlayment as a resilient floor base.

Sheets of untempered hardboard, plywood, or particleboard, which are 4 × 4 feet or larger and 1/4 or 1/8 inch thick are used in remodeling work because of the floor thickness involved. The underlayment grade of particleboard is a standard product and is available from many building material retailers. Manufacturer's instructions should be followed in the care and use of the product.

Plywood underlayment is also a common product and is available in an interior, exterior, and interior type with an interior glue line. The underlayment grade provides for a sanded panel with a C-plugged or better grade immediately under the face. This construction resists damage to the floor surface from concentrated loads such as chair legs and heavy furniture.

Generally, underlayment panels are separate and are installed over structurally adequate subfloors. Combination subfloor underlayment panels of plywood construction are being used with increasing frequency. Panels for this dual purpose generally have tongue-and-groove or blocked edges and C-plugged or better faces, which provide a smooth, even surface for the resilient floor covering. To prevent nails from showing on the surface of the tile, joists and subfloors should have a moisture content that is near the average value they will reach after installing.

The thickness of the underlayment will vary somewhat, depending on the floors in adjoining rooms. Kitchen tile, for example, is usually installed on 5/8-inch underlayment when finish floors in the adjoining living or dining areas are 25/32-inch strip flooring (FIG. 2-2). When thinner wood floors are used in adjoining rooms, adjustments are made in the thickness of the underlayment.

Concrete that will have resilient floors installed on it should be prepared with a good vapor barrier somewhere between the soil and the finish floor, preferably just under the slab. Concrete should be leveled carefully when a resilient floor is to be used directly on the slab so dips and waves are minimized.

Tile shouldn't be laid on a concrete slab until it has completely dried. One method that may be used to determine if the concrete has dried is to place a small square of polyethylene or other low-perm material on the slab overnight. If the underside is dry in the morning, the slab is usually considered dry enough for the installation of tile.

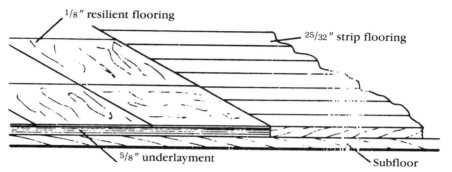

2-2 Resilient flooring can also be laid over underlayment to butt strip flooring.

CERAMIC TILE BASES

Ceramic floor tiles can be installed over a variety of bases, including concrete and wood. Figures 2-3 through 2-14 illustrate a variety of suggested installation methods on different bases. The adhesives used will be discussed later in this chapter.

Ceramic tile and similar floor coverings may be installed by the cement-plaster method or with adhesives. The cement-plaster method requires a concrete-cement setting bed of $1\frac{1}{4}$ inch minimum thickness (FIG. 2-3). Joists are beveled and cleats used to support the waterproof, plywood subfloor or forms are cut between the joists. The cement base is reinforced with woven-wire fabric or expanded metal lath.

Ceramic tile is normally soaked before it is installed. It is pressed firmly in place in the still-plastic setting bed, then mortar is compressed into the joints. The joints are tooled the same day tile is laid. Laying tile in this manner normally requires a workman skilled in this system. In Chapter 4 you will learn the method used by most do-it-yourselfers.

Adhesive used for ceramic floor tile should be the type recommended by the manufacturer. When ceramic tile is to be installed over wood joists, a waterproof plywood that is $3/4$ inch thick and has been perimeter and intermediate nailed provides a good base. Before you install tile, a waterproof sealer or a thin coat of tile adhesive must be applied to the plywood.

Tile is best set over a full covering of adhesive. Use the floating method with a slight twisting movement for full embedment. Buttering, or using small pats of adhesive on each tile, is not acceptable. Tile should not be grouted or joints filled until volatiles from the adhesive have evaporated. After grouting, joints should be fully tooled.

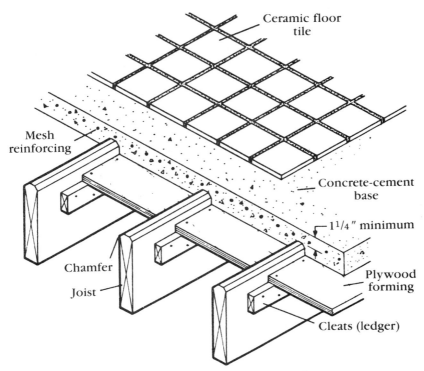

Ceramic floor tile

Mesh reinforcing

Concrete-cement base

1¹/₄" minimum

Chamfer

Joist

Plywood forming

Cleats (ledger)

2-3   Ceramic tile installed on a cement base.

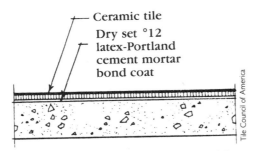

Ceramic tile

Dry set °12 latex-Portland cement mortar bond coat

Tile Council of America

2-4   Dry-set mortar over a concrete subfloor.

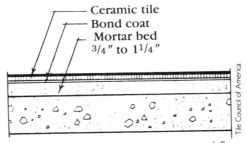

Ceramic tile
Bond coat
Mortar bed
³/₄" to 1¹/₄"

Tile Council of America

2-5   Cement mortar over a concrete subfloor.

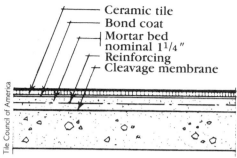

Ceramic tile
Bond coat
Mortar bed
nominal 1¹/₄″
Reinforcing
Cleavage membrane

Tile Council of America

2-6 Cement mortar over a reinforced concrete subfloor.

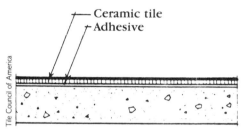

Ceramic tile
Adhesive

Tile Council of America

2-7 Organic or epoxy adhesive over a concrete slab.

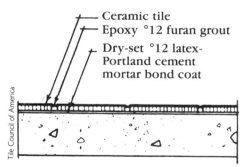

Ceramic tile
Epoxy °12 furan grout
Dry-set °12 latex-
Portland cement
mortar bond coat

Tile Council of America

2-8 Dry-set mortar and epoxy grout over a concrete subfloor.

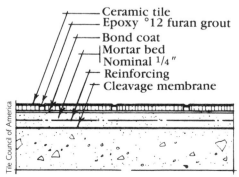

Ceramic tile
Epoxy °12 furan grout
Bond coat
Mortar bed
Nominal ¹/₄″
Reinforcing
Cleavage membrane

Tile Council of America

2-9 Cement mortar and epoxy grout over a concrete subfloor.

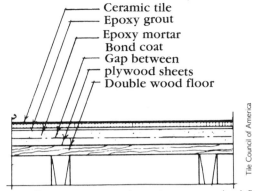

Ceramic tile
Epoxy grout
Epoxy mortar
Bond coat
Gap between
plywood sheets
Double wood floor

Tile Council of America

2-10   Epoxy mortar and grout over wood subfloor.

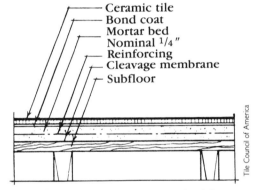

Ceramic tile
Bond coat
Mortar bed
Nominal 1/4"
Reinforcing
Cleavage membrane
Subfloor

Tile Council of America

2-11   Cement mortar over wood subfloor.

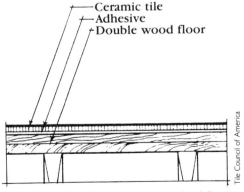

Ceramic tile
Adhesive
Double wood floor

Tile Council of America

2-12   Organic adhesive over wood subfloor.

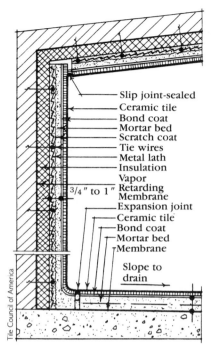

2-13 Installing ceramic tile in a steam room.

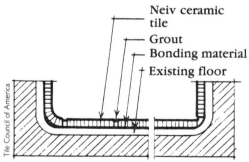

2-14 Installing ceramic tile over an existing floor.

Again, this general information on installing a tile floor is offered as an overview to guide you in planning your floor. Specific instructions will be offered in Chapters 3 and 4.

ESTIMATING TILE NEEDS

A simple square or rectangular room requires only minimal math to estimate the amount of floor tile needed. The length of the room is multiplied by the width (i.e., 9 × 12 feet) in order to find out the total floor area (108 square feet). It is then a matter of knowing the size and spacing of the selected tiles.

Many rooms, however, are not as simple to estimate. Figures 2-15 through 2-19 and TABLE 2-1 illustrate how various rooms can be measured easily for square footage. Figures 2-20 through 2-30 illustrate how to estimate the size of walls, showers, and countertops to be tiled.

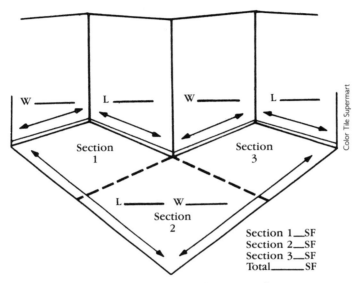

2-15   Measuring a room for quarry tile.

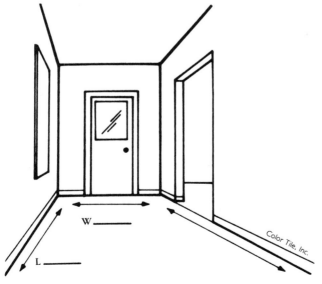

2-16   Measuring a hallway for quarry tile.

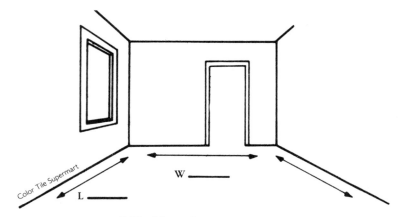

2-17   Measuring a square room.

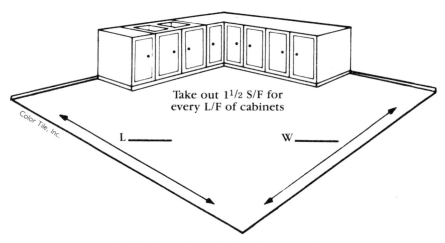

2-18   Measuring a kitchen for floor tile.

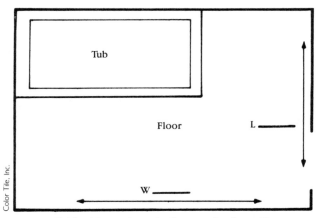

2-19   Measuring a bathroom for floor tile.

Table 2-1   Ceramic Tile Estimating Table.

Example _____
FLOOR: W _____ × _____ L = _____ S/F
FLOOR: W _____ × _____ L = _____ S/F
FLOOR: W _____ × _____ L = _____ S/F
FLOOR: W _____ × _____ L = _____ S/F
FLOOR: W _____ × _____ L = _____ S/F
NOTE: Subtract 12 S/F for tub _____ S/F
        TOTAL: _____

NOTE:
4 × 8 = 11 S/F per carton: 4.5 Pcs. Per S/F
6 × 6 = 11 S/F per carton: 4 Pcs. Per S/F
8 × 8 = 11 S/F per carton: 2.25 Pcs. Per S/F
10 × 10 = 11 S/F per carton: 1.44 Pcs. Per S/F
12 × 12 = 11 S/F per carton: 1 Pc. Per S/F
NOTE: If figuring with inches: Total inches ÷ by 144
        = S/F "Tile"

Total inches ÷ by 12
        = L/F "Trim"

Color Tile Supermart

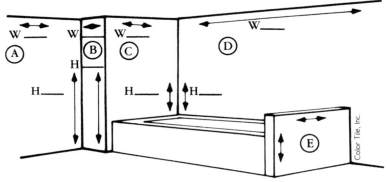

2-20 Measuring a bathroom for ceramic wall tile.

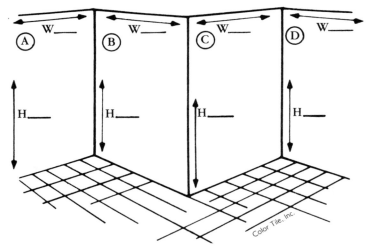

2-21 Measuring short walls for ceramic tile.

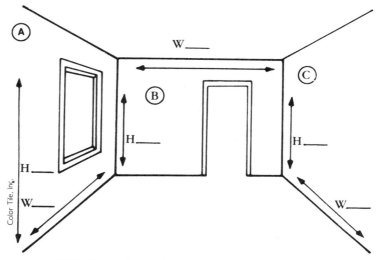

2-22 Measuring typical room for ceramic wall tile.

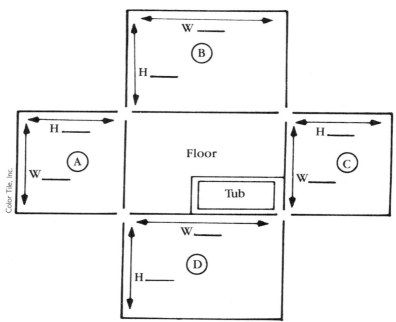

2-23 Layout of a bathroom for ceramic wall tile.

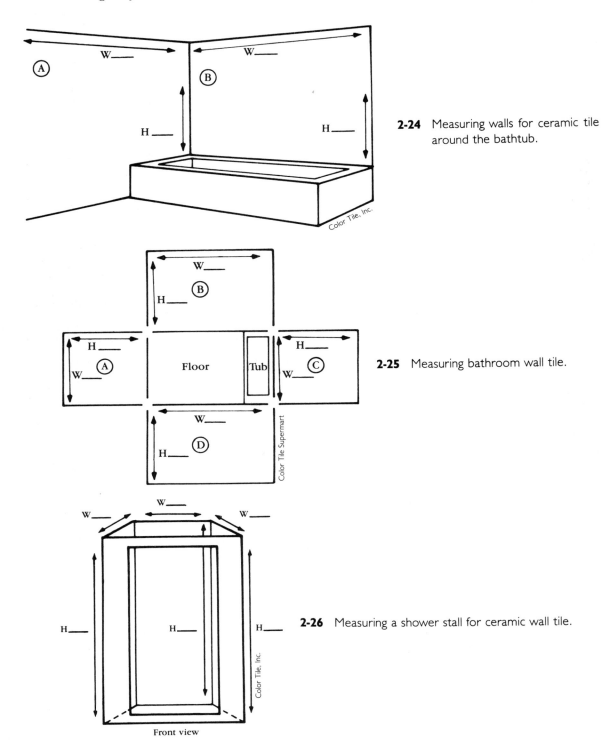

2-24 Measuring walls for ceramic tile around the bathtub.

2-25 Measuring bathroom wall tile.

2-26 Measuring a shower stall for ceramic wall tile.

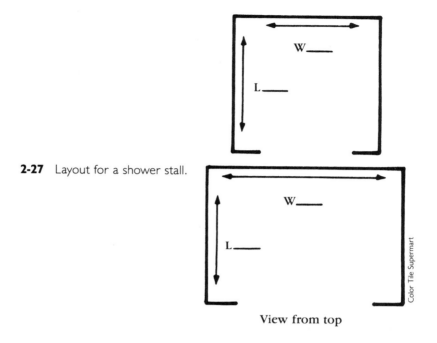

2-27 Layout for a shower stall.

View from top

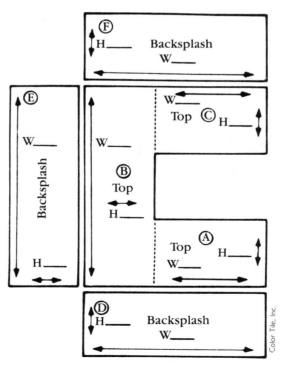

2-28 Layout of kitchen countertop for ceramic tile.

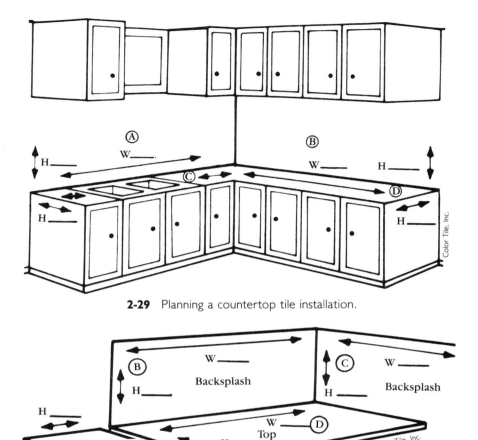

2-29   Planning a countertop tile installation.

2-30   Layout of a straight-run countertop.

SELECTING TILE TOOLS

There are a number of general and specialized tools available to aid in the installation of resilient and hard tile floors. Many are so specialized that they are difficult to find except in the tool boxes of professional tile installers. Fortunately, new tile designs and manufacturing methods have made such tools nearly obsolete and rarely vital to the do-it-yourselfer. Most of the tools you will need are either in your shop now or readily available.

You can also purchase the tools you need individually. Figure 2-31 illustrates the chalk line, a tool common to a variety of do-it-yourself jobs, and therefore likely to be in many tool boxes. Perhaps the most convenient type of chalk line is the kind with a metal box or case. The box keeps the line clean when it is not in use and also holds an ample supply

2-31 Chalk line used for marking floor prior to tile installation.

of chalk, which adheres to the line as it is pulled from the box. After use, the line may be returned to the box by means of a small crank or winding handle. The box or case may also serve as a plumb bob.

The chalk line is used to mark finish and working lines when tile is being installed. The line is stretched tightly between two predetermined points and then lifted near the center and allowed to snap back against the surface, when it deposits a thin line of chalk dust. The dust can readily be removed from most surfaces when it is no longer needed.

In order to do efficient work, the do-it-yourself tile setter should have at least one level (FIG. 2-32). The 24-inch level is the most convenient and will work for most jobs. In some cases, though, a smaller, 9-inch level will be valuable. When working on large areas, a 48-inch mason's level will give more accuracy and save considerable time.

The level must be checked for accuracy from time to time, particularly if it is an adjustable one. Jarring and pounding on the level will impair its accuracy, and make adjustments necessary. The simplest way to check a level is to reverse it. If the reading is the same either way, there is no need for adjustment. The level should never be hit with another tool, nor should it ever be used as a screed for leveling off mortar.

The combination square is a small square with an adjustable head. It usually has a 1 × 12-inch blade grooved to fit the keeper in the head of the square. A thumbscrew adjustment permits you to lock the head at any

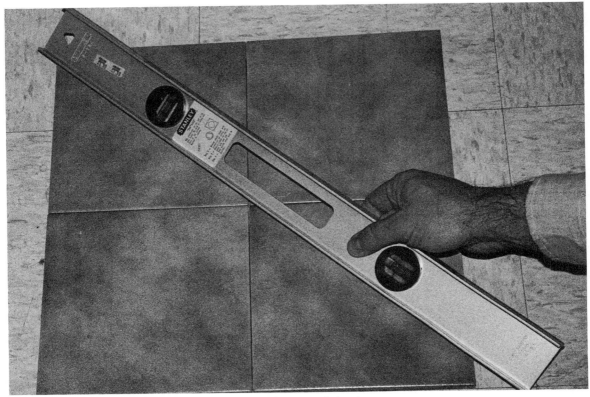

2-32 Carpenter's level.

point along the blade. The long part of the head is at right angles to the blade. Opposite this is a beveled side that forms a 45-degree angle with the blade. High-grade squares have a level glass placed just above the margin of the long side of the head. At the end of the head, opposite the blade, is often a small scriber. This piece is fitted with a rounded knob to facilitate withdrawing it from the head. The scriber is useful in marking metal and other hard surfaces, such as tile.

The claw hammer is another common tool that is used by the tile installer. It is used for nailing on paper and metal lath, installing subflooring, and chipping. A chipping hammer can also be used to chip away excess materials from the back of the tile and along the edges.

The pry bar (FIG. 2-33) is used primarily to pry tiles apart or to remove old flooring materials. Figure 2-34 illustrates three tile cutting tools. Tile nippers (FIG. 2-35) look much like the carpenter's nail pullers. You can even use a nail puller if you don't have tile nippers. The tile nipper is used to take small bites out of ceramic and other hard tiles. Remember to only take small bites with the tile nippers because big bites may cause the tile to crack and break. It is usually best to score the tile either with a glass cutter or a tile cutting board before attempting the cut.

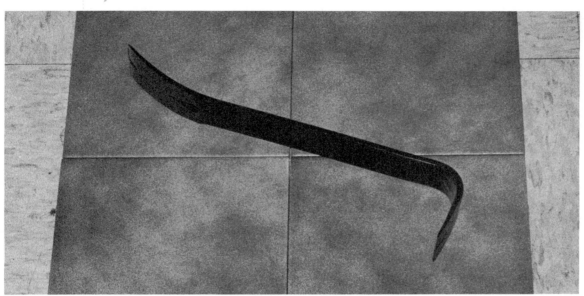

2-33 Pry bar.

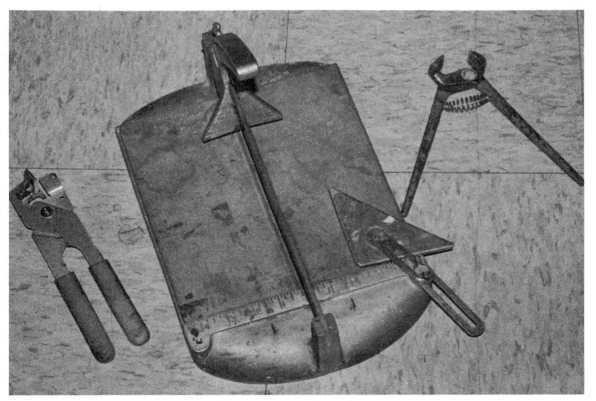

2-34 Three common tile-cutting tools.

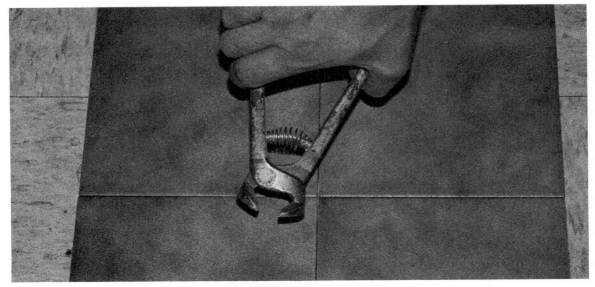

2-35 Tile nippers.

The tile cutter (FIG. 2-36) is one of the most efficient and economical tools for cutting hard tiles. One type consists of an aluminum base with a steel bar above. It has a slotted handle that is fitted with a glass cutter cluster that slides back and forth as the cut is made. The clusters usually consist of three or six tiny wheels that may be fitted with a rib in the center, which is in line with the cutters. The breaking bar exerts pressure over this rib to break the scored tile. Rubber pads at each side of the center rib provide cushions to reduce the shock and help prevent the tile from breaking in any direction except that desired. The slotted part of the handle and the steel guide should be slightly oiled to keep the action free. The board is equipped with an angle gauge for 45- and 90-degree angles. Other angles may be obtained by adjusting the gauge to the cut desired.

An electric tile saw is also available, but is usually not used by the do-it-yourselfer. Tile cutters may also be rented or borrowed from tile stores.

Figure 2-37 illustrates a tile snapper. The snapper will break the typical ceramic tile along the score line when it is depressed.

Figure 2-38 shows a typical grout trowel that is used to wipe excess grout from tile surfaces. There are many other types of trowels that spread the adhesives and grouts that are used in tile installation.

Those are the most common tools used to install tile flooring. Most of them are made specifically for the installation of hard tiles because resilient tile flooring is much simpler to install and usually requires little more than a chalk line, some snips, and possibly an adhesive spreader. In many cases, the tiles are self adhering which makes the job easy.

Probably the most difficult task for the do-it-yourself tile installer is cutting hard tiles. Let's consider the best ways to make professional cuts.

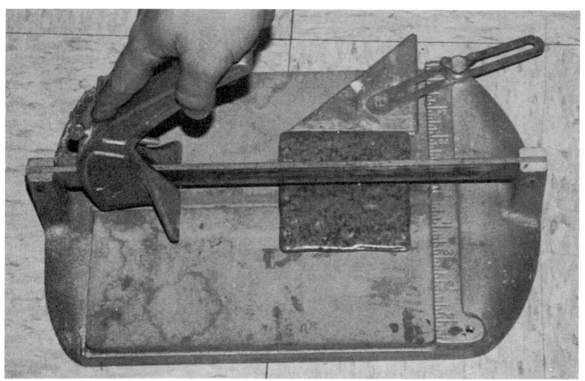

2-36   Tile cutter ready to score the tile.

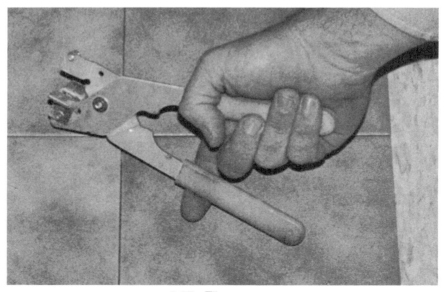

2-37   Tile snappers.

2-38   Tile grout trowel.

CUTTING TILE

If there is no tile saw or cutting board available, tile may be cut with a glass cutter. The glass cutter gives you two pieces, whereas if the tile is cut with a tile nipper, only one piece is obtained.

The tools you'll need include a glass cutter, a steel rule, and a chisel. First, place a straightedge along the cut line. Next, hold the glass cutter upright and bring it toward you along the edge of the straightedge. Be sure that the straightedge doesn't slip. Now make only one cut along the desired line. Repeated scoring will tend to chip the glaze too much. After you've scored the tile, break it over a chisel.

When it's necessary to cut a small amount off the edges of the tile in order to make them fit in a given area, use the tile nippers. The same job can be done with the tile saw, if you have one.

You'll need tile nippers, a pencil, and a folding rule to trim the tile with the nippers. First, mark the line along which the tile is to be cut. Next, hold the tile with your left hand and grip the tile with the jaws of the nippers. Put the jaws of the nipper on the tile at half its width, rather than taking a full bite. Now hold the lower jaw of the nippers slightly forward. Exert a little downward pressure on the handles as you squeeze them together. This will tend to break the tile chips on a bevel and away from the line of the cut.

Cut the tile carefully to avoid excessive grinding. Taking bites that are too large will cause the tile to break in the wrong direction. It is better to take a small bite each time and work up to the desired line. This will help when you are making a notched cut, which you must do when installing hard tile around pipes or other plumbing.

The tile cutter is a mechanical device that has guides and scoring wheels. It reduces the time needed to cut hard tile. To cut with the tile cutter, place the tile at the back edge of the cutter and against the rear guide. Next, move the adjustable gauge to the side of the tile and lock it when the mark for the cut is directly below the cutting wheel. Then grasp the handle firmly with your right hand and, beginning at the edge farthest from you, bring the cutter toward you. The result will be a neat score that needs only to be broken.

The handle of the tile cutter has an extension at the bottom that runs at right angles to the handle itself. This is the breaking bar. The narrow rib that runs parallel with and directly beneath the guide bar serves the same purpose as a chisel. Press down on the handle until the breaking bar is touching the tile. Then, with a quick press, continue the movement downward. The tile will break neatly along the desired line, if it is scored deeply enough and aligned properly with the breaking rip. Make both parallel and diagonal cuts in this manner because guides are provided for these various types of cuts.

ADHESIVES

There are numerous adhesives available for the installation of resilient and hard tile flooring (TABLE 2-2). Basically, mortar is a combination of sand, cement, either fireclay or lime, and water. It's primarily used as a thick adhesive into which hard tiles are set. Tile adhesive is a thinner substance that is spread on the subfloor. Resilient or hard tile is laid directly on the adhesive. Some types of resilient tile have a self-adhesive on the underside, which can be activated by simply pealing off a cover sheet. Grout is a thin, course mortar that is used to fill the space between the hard tiles.

While the selection of mortar, adhesive and grout will be dictated by the type of tile flooring you select, as well as manufacturers' and retailers' suggestions, you should know what's available and how they work. Let's take mortar, adhesive, and grout separately.

TILE MORTAR

There are six common types of mortar that are used in the installation of hard tiles. Each having its own unique properties and applications.

Portland cement mortar A mixture of portland cement and sand is used on floors, and a combination of portland cement, sand, and lime is used for walls. Portland cement mortar is suitable for most surfaces and ordinary types of installation. The thick setting bed, which is $3/4$ to 1 inch on walls and $3/4$ to $1^{1}/4$ inches on floors, facilitates accurate slopes or planes in the finished tile work. Proportions are given on the packages.

Dry-set mortar A mixture of portland cement sand, and additives that impart water retentivity is usually used as a bond coat for setting tile. Dry-set mortar is suitable for use over a variety of surfaces. It is used in one

Table 2-2 Grout Guide

GROUT GUIDE

Printed through the courtesy of the Materials & Methods Standards Association A rubber faced trowel should be used when grouting glazed tile with sanded grout.		GROUT TYPE									
		Commercial Portland Cement		Sand-Portland Cement	Dry-Set	Latex Port-land Cement (3)	Mastic (3)	Epoxy (1) (6)	Furan (1) (6)	Silicone or Urethane (2)	Modified Epoxy Emulsion (3) (6)
		Wall Use	Floor Use	Wall-Floor Use	Wall-Floor Use						
TILE TYPE	GLAZED WALL TILE (More than 7% absorption)	•			•	•	•			•	
	CERAMIC MOSAICS	⊙	•	•	•	•		•		•	•
	QUARRY, PAVER & PACKING HOUSE TILE	•	•	•		•		•	•		•
AREAS OF USE	Dry and intermittently wet areas	•	•	•	•	•	•	•	•	•	•
	Areas subject to prolonged wetting	•	•	•	•	•		•	•	•	•
	Exteriors	•	•	•	•	•(4)		•(4)	•(4)		•(4)
PERFORMANCE	Stain Resistance (5)	D	C	E	D	B	A	A	A	A	B
	Crack Resistance (5)	D	D	E	D	C	C	B	C	A Flexible	C
	Colorability (5)	B	B	C	B	B	A	B	Black Only	Restricted	B

Tile Council of America

(1) Mainly used for chemical resistant properties.
(2) Special tools needed for proper application. Silicone, urethane and modified polyvinylchloride used in pregrouted ceramic tile sheets. Silicone grout should not be used on kitchen countertops or other food preparation surfaces unless it meets the requirements of FDA Regulation No. 21, CFE 177.2600.
(3) Special cleaning procedures and materials recommended.
(4) Follow manufacturer's directions.
(5) Five performance ratings — Best to Minimal (A B C D E).
(6) Epoxies are recommended for prolonged temperatures up to 140F, high temperature resistant epoxies and furans up to 350F.

layer, which can be as thin as 3/32 inch. After the tiles are beat in, dry-set mortar has excellent water and impact resistance, can be cleaned with water, is nonflammable, is good for exterior work, and doesn't require the tiles to be soaked before installation.

Latex-portland cement mortar This mortar is a mixture of portland cement, sand, and a special latex additive that is used as a bond coat for setting tile. The uses for latex-portland cement mortar are similar to those of dry-set mortar. It is less rigid than portland cement mortar. Latex-portland cement mortar is used to install ceramic tile in areas that may not thoroughly dry out in use, such as swimming pools and gang showers. It is recommended that the completed installation be allowed to dry thoroughly before it is exposed to water. This drying period can fluctuate from 14 to over 60 days, depending upon the geographical location, the climate conditions, and whether the installation is interior or exterior.

Epoxy mortar Epoxy is a mortar system that employs epoxy resin and epoxy hardener portions. Epoxy mortar is suitable for use where the chemical resistance of floors, high bond strength, and high impact resistance are important considerations. Acceptable subfloors, when properly prepared, include concrete, wood, plywood, steel plate, and ceramic tile. Application is made in one thin layer.

Modified epoxy emulsion mortars   This is a mortar/grout system that employs emulsified epoxy resins and hardeners with portland cement and silica sand. Modified epoxy emulsion mortars are formulated for thinset ceramic tile installations on interior and exterior floors and walls. Their features include high-bond strength, ease of application, little or no shrinkage, and economical epoxy application. These mortars are not designed for chemical epoxy application. They are not designed for chemical resistance, but are better than portland cement mortars or organic adhesives. Recommended uses include residential and light-duty floors over substrates such as plywood and concrete. This material is recommended by most manufacturers as a bond coat or setting material. Some also recommend it for grouting. Properties vary with the manufacturer.

Furan mortar   This mortar system consists of furan resin and furan hardener portions. Furan mortar is suitable for use where the chemical resistance of floors is an important consideration. Acceptable subfloors, when properly prepared, include concrete, wood, steel plate, and ceramic tile. Properties vary with the manufacturer.

TILE ADHESIVES

There are basically two types of adhesive used in the installation of tile: epoxy and organic.

Epoxy adhesive   The epoxy adhesive system employs epoxy resin and epoxy hardener portions. Epoxy adhesive is formulated for the thinsetting of tile on floors, walls, and counters with epoxy as the major binder. It is designed primarily for high-bond strength and its ease of application, not for optimum chemical resistance. Its chemical and solvent resistance, however, tends to be better than that of organic adhesives.

Organic adhesive   This is a system of prepared organic material that is ready to use without additional liquids or powders, and that cures or sets by evaporation. Organic adhesive is suitable for installing tile on floors, walls, and counters. It should be applied in one thin layer with a trowel. First use the flat edge of the trowel for continuous coverage and then the notched edge for uniform thickness. Where leveling or truing is required, an underlayment should be used.

Adhesives eliminate the need for the tile to be soaked. They are not suitable for swimming pools or exteriors, but are often used for residential floors. They supply some flexibility to the tile facing. Bond strength varies greatly among the numerous brands available.

TILE GROUTS

Grouting materials for ceramic tile are available in many forms to meet the requirements of the different kinds of tile and types of exposures. Portland cement is the base for most grouts and is modified to provide specific qualities such as whiteness, mildew resistance, uniformity, hardness, flexibility, and water retentivity. Non-cement-based grouts, such as epoxies, furans, and silicon rubber, offer properties that are not possible with cement grouts. Special skills on the part of the setter are often required.

Commercial portland cement grout   A mixture of portland cement and other ingredients in this grout produces a water-resistant, dense, uniformly colored material. Floor grout, which is usually gray, is designed for use with ceramic mosaics, quarry, and paver tiles. The wall type, which is usually white, is designed for conventional mortar installations with a very fine variety of aggregate. Damp curing is required for both floor and wall types.

Sand-portland cement grout   This is an on-the-job grout mixture. One part portland cement to 1 part fine graded sand is used for joints up to $1/8$ inch wide; a ratio of 1:2 is used for joints up to $1/2$ inch wide. Up to $1/5$ part lime may be added. Sand-portland cement grout is used with ceramic mosaic tile, quarry, and paver tile on floors and walls. Damp curing is necessary.

Dry-set grout   A mixture of portland cement and additives that provides water retentivity, dry-set grout has the same characteristics as dry-set mortar described earlier. It is suitable for grouting all floors and walls subject to ordinary use. This grout eliminates the soaking of tile, although dampening is sometimes required under very dry conditions. Damp curing may develop greater strength in portland cement grouts.

Latex-portland cement grout   This is a mixture of any one of the three preceding grouts with a special latex additive. Latex-portland cement grout is suitable for all hard tile installations that are subject to ordinary use and for most commercial installations. It is less absorptive than regular cement grout.

Mastic grout   A one-part grouting composition that is used directly from the container, mastic grout hardens by coalescence and doesn't require damp curing as do the portland cement-based grouts. It is more flexible and stain-resistant than regular cement grout.

Furan resin grout   A grout system consisting of furan resin and hardener portions, this grout is used primarily for quarry tile, packing-house tile, and paver tile. Furan grout is used in industrial and commercial areas that require chemical resistance. The use of this grout involves extra costs, including the waxing of tile surfaces, and special installation skills when compared to portland cement grouts.

Epoxy grout   This grouting system employs epoxy resin and hardener portions and often contains coarse silica filler. It is especially formulated for industrial and commercial installations. This grout provides chemical resistance, high-bond strength, and impact resistance. High-temperature/chemical-resistant formulas are also available. They impart structural qualities to the tile when used both as a mortar and grout, especially over wood subfloors. They are more expensive to install than portland cement grouts.

Silicon rubber grout An engineered elastometric grout system for interior use, silicon rubber grout employs a single component of nonslumping silicon rubber. When cured, it is resistant to staining, moisture, mildew, cracking, crazing, and shrinking. This grout adheres tenaciously to ceramic tile without primers, cures rapidly, and withstands exposure to hot cooking oils, free steam, and oxygen, as well as prolonged exposure to subfreezing temperatures and hot humid conditions. Silicon rubber grout is more costly, but can be very practical for many floor and wall installations.

RESILIENT TILE ADHESIVES

Adhesives for resilient tile vary greatly depending on the composition of the tile itself and the subfloor on which it is to be applied. In many cases, such as self-stick resilient tiles, the selection of the correct adhesive is made for you. In other cases, the adhesive is suggested by the manufacturer or the retailer. It is best to take this advice, which was developed through chemical testing and laboratory application. If possible, stay with the brand suggested by the manufacturer because each brand will have a slightly different composition and may react differently when applied.

Chapter **3**

Installing resilient tile floors

Resilient tile floors are the most popular with the do-it-yourselfer because they are easy to install. They are also less expensive than hard-tile or wood floors. The typical cost of resilient tile floors is $75 to $125 per room.

Resilient tile floors come in two types, which are defined by the method of installation or adhesion. Self-adhering tile flooring has a backing that can be pulled away to expose an adhesive. Dry-back tile must have the adhesive spread on the floor or the back of the tile. Otherwise, installation is very similar.

REMOVING THE EXISTING FLOOR

The first step in the installation of a resilient tile floor is the removal of any existing flooring. This step isn't required for new construction or an add-on room. Carpeting can be pulled up easily and tack strips removed, but in many cases, an earlier resilient tile or sheet flooring must be removed.

First, a word of warning: don't sand existing flooring, backing, or lining felt. These products may contain asbestos fibers that are not readily identifiable. Inhalation of asbestos dust may damage lungs, especially if you also smoke.

To remove existing sheet flooring, the wear layer should first be cut into narrow strips. Be careful not to score the underlayment if it is a wood subfloor. The narrow strips should then be peeled off from the backing by pulling or rolling around a core. A core will control the stripping angle and create uniform tension. You may not be able to strip some resilient flooring, but may have to scrape it instead.

After the wear layer has been removed, examine the remaining felt to determine whether or not it will serve as a suitable base for the new floor covering. Areas where the felt has not adhered should be cut open and rebound. Areas where the backing pulls free should be leveled with a latex underlayment.

If the remaining felt is not suitable, it should be removed by wet scraping. Moisten the felt with a water solution of dishwashing detergent. The solution should be applied to the felt backing and allowed to penetrate for several minutes before you scrape. Only enough solution should be used to keep the top surface of the backing damp. More than one application may be necessary, therefore, depending upon the time required for removal.

Proper care must be exercised in the cleanup and disposal of all waste material when you remove resilient flooring. The material should be placed in heavy-duty plastic trash bags or similar containers to minimize dust generation. Exposed floor areas should be cleaned with a wet-dry vacuum cleaner.

Remember not to soak the felt because excessive moisture can cause permanent damage to the wood underlayment. A floor that has been wet-scraped must be allowed to dry before you install the resilient flooring.

INSTALLING SELF-ADHERING TILE

The installation of self-adhering, or self-stick, resilient floor tile is very simple (FIG. 3-1). For the best color match when using tiles from two or more packages, check to be sure all pattern and lot numbers are the same.

For proper installation, floors must be smooth and completely free of wax, grease, and dirt. Dusty concrete subfloors should be vacuumed. Firmly bonded paint and smooth-surface resilient floors are acceptable bases for self-adhering floor tiles. Embossed no-wax urethane floors or cushioned floors are not acceptable and should be removed.

Particleboard, frequently called chipboard, is sometimes used as a type of underlayment. Results of the bonding may not be satisfactory, however, so many manufacturers recommend that you do not lay self-adhering tile flooring over particleboard. In most cases, you can install such flooring over suspended, on-grade, and below-grade floors, and over terrazzo floors.

3-1 Typical installation of vinyl self-adhering floor tile.

Never install flooring tiles over a subfloor that is wet or damp. The surface of the subfloor must be dry to insure a good adhesive bond. Install in an area with a minimum temperature of 65 degrees Fahrenheit for at least 48 hours before and during installation and for 48 hours after installation. Thereafter, a minimum temperature of 55 degrees should be maintained to help establish a firm bond to the subfloor.

First, pry up molding at the base of walls so that tiles can be placed underneath during installation. Next, find the center for each of the end walls. Connect these points by striking a chalk line down the middle of the floor. This is the center chalk line (FIG. 3-2).

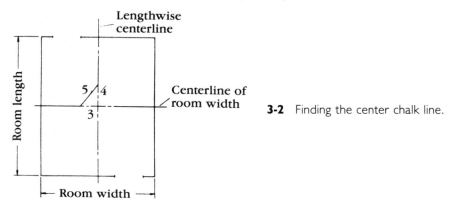

3-2 Finding the center chalk line.

Locate the center of this line. Now, using a tile, draw a perpendicular line. On this perpendicular line, strike a chalk line connecting the two sidewalls. The floor is now divided into quarters (FIG. 3-3). Next, place a row of tiles along the perpendicular chalk line from the center of the room to the sidewall, but don't remove the release paper (FIG. 3-4).

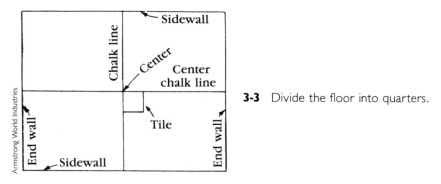

3-3 Divide the floor into quarters.

Measure the distance between the sidewall and the last full tile. If the space is less than half the width of a tile, strike a new chalk line beside the old center chalk line half the width of a tile either toward or away from the wall. This will give even borders on both sides of the room. Repeat the procedure on the end wall. The point where the two chalk lines cross is the starting point for installing tiles (FIG. 3-5).

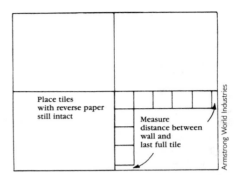

3-4 Laying self-adhering floor tiles.

Place tiles with reverse paper still intact

Measure distance between wall and last full tile

Armstrong World Industries

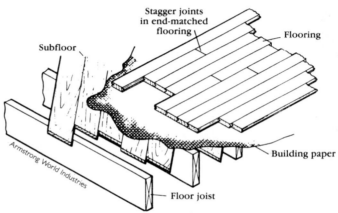

Stagger joints in end-matched flooring

Flooring

Subfloor

Building paper

Armstrong World Industries

Floor joist

3-5 Adjust chalk line before beginning the installation.

Now remove the release paper from each tile as you install it (FIG. 3-6). Start placing tiles at the center point. Make sure that the edges are even with the chalk line and that each tile is butted against adjoining pieces (FIG. 3-7). Do not slide the tiles into place. Press the tiles firmly into place as you install them. For the best appearance, install each embossed tile with the arrows on the back all pointing in the same direction (FIG. 3-8). Cover the first quarter of the room with the exception of the border area where the tiles must be cut to fit.

To cut and fit the tiles next to the walls, place a loose tile (FIG. 3-9A) exactly on top of the last full tile in any row. On top of this, place a third tile (FIG. 3-9B) and slide it until it butts against the wall. Using the edge of the top as a guide, mark the tile under it with a pencil. Then use a straight-blade utility knife or a sturdy pair of household shears (FIG. 3-10) to cut along this line. To fit pieces of tile around pipes or other irregularities, make a pattern of the proper shape from paper, trace it on the tile, and cut.

Finally, repeat these steps for the remaining three quarters of the room. In just a few hours the job is completed, and your room has a new resilient tile floor (FIG. 3-11).

3-6 Peel off the protective paper for installation.

3-7 Maneuver the tile into position.

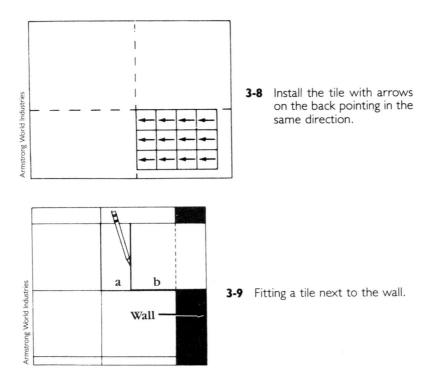

3-8 Install the tile with arrows on the back pointing in the same direction.

3-9 Fitting a tile next to the wall.

INSTALLING DRY-BACK TILE

The installation procedures for a dry-back resilient tile floor is much the same as that for a self-adhering tile floor. Make sure that your base floor or subfloor is ready for installation, that the old flooring (if any) is removed or prepared, and that the area is clean. These steps will ensure good adhesion of the new flooring tiles.

To locate the center of the room, find the center of each wall, then pull a chalked strip taut to the opposite wall across the center of the room. Snap a straight line on the subfloor so that the room is squared off and so that the tile is laid parallel to the walls.

To plan the floor, lay a row of loose tiles along the chalk line from the center point to one side wall and one end wall. Measure the distance between the wall and the last full tile. If this space is less than a half a tile wide, snap a new chalk line and move half a width of tile closer to the opposite wall. Check the right angles. Now, do the same with the other row. This will improve the appearance of the floor and eliminate the need to fit small pieces of tile next to the walls.

Check to make sure that you have the correct adhesive for your tile. Before spreading the adhesive, read the instruction label on the can. Spread the adhesive over one quarter of the area, which is bounded on two sides by the center chalk lines. Adhesive should be brushed, troweled, or rolled on thinly so that when the tile is laid, the adhesive will not push up between the tiles or cause them to slip underfoot.

3-10 Using household shears to cut the tile.

3-11 The completed self-adhering resilient tile floor.

Allow the adhesive to set the recommended time. Then, starting at the center point, lay the tile in the adhesive (FIG. 3-12). Lay one quarter section of the room at a time. Start at the center point and move toward one wall (FIG. 3-13). Each tile should be set down firmly and tightly against the adjoining tile so that there are no joints between the tiles. Don't slide the tiles into place or the adhesive may come up between the tiles.

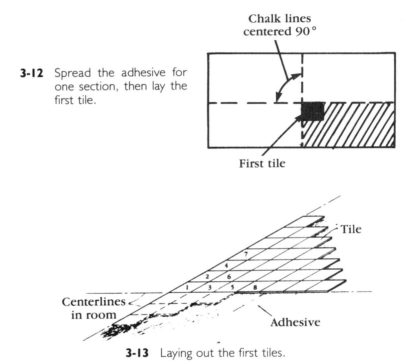

3-12 Spread the adhesive for one section, then lay the first tile.

3-13 Laying out the first tiles.

To cut and fit the dry-back tile next to the wall, place a loose tile (FIG. 3-14A) squarely on top of the last full tile that is closest to the wall. On top of this, place a third tile (FIG. 3-14B) and slide it until it butts against the wall. Using the edge of the top tile as a guide, mark the tile under it with a pencil. With a pair of household shears, cut tile A along the pencil line.

To fit around pipes and other obstructions, make a paper pattern to fit the space exactly. Trace the outline onto the tile and cut with the shears. Insert tile into the border space with the rough edge against the wall (FIG. 3-15).

INSTALLING SHEET FLOORING

Installing sheet flooring is very easy for the do-it-yourselfer. First, prepare the floor. Nail all loose boards, replace defective boards, fill cracks with wood filler, and remove all dirt, grease, wax, varnish, and paint. You may have to remove the previous flooring.

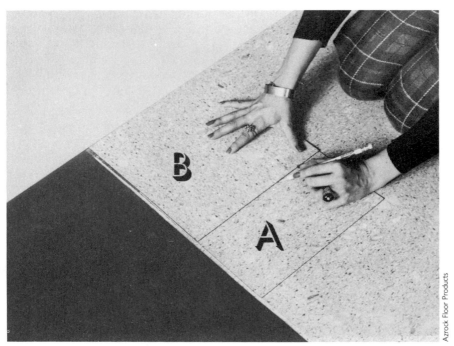

3-14   Fitting tiles next to the wall.

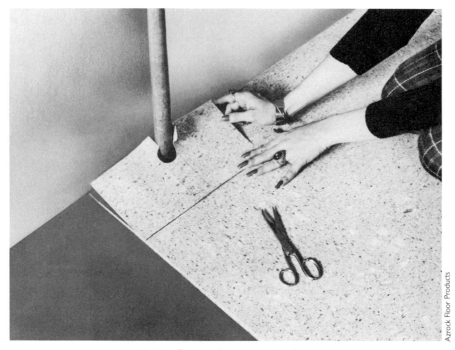

3-15   Fitting tiles around a pipe.

Felt can be laid first to increase the life of the flooring covering. Unroll the first strips across the floor boards, not along the boards. Cut strips to fit around pipes, other projections, and baseboards at each end. Butt the second strip to the first. Never overlap. When strips have been fitted to the whole room, roll them all back halfway. Spread adhesive on the floor with a spreader to the thickness recommended by the manufacturer. Then roll the felt strips back over the paste and repeat the adhesive application for the other half of the room. After all felt is pasted, roll it with a rolling pin, putting your body weight heavily on it. Leave the felt to set for two or three hours before you lay sheet flooring. Note that concrete floors should not have felt.

Standard sheet flooring many times comes in rolls that are 72 inches wide. The piece to be fitted runs from end to end of the room and butts side baseboards.

First, unroll the sheet flooring across the floor boards and parallel to the felt, if any. Next, cut the piece at least 2 inches longer than the room. Then place the piece so it rides up 1 inch on each end baseboard. Now pull the piece out from the side baseboard so it lies flat.

Strap chalk to the inside of one leg of the carpenter's dividers with tape. Set the dividers so that the sharp point sets firmly at the joint between the baseboard and floor. The chalk point should rest 1 inch inside the edge of the sheet. Start at one end of the sheet and draw a chalk line the whole length (FIG. 3-16). Now cut the sheet flooring along the line.

An alternate method is to lay paper out on the floor. Stick the paper to the floor by cutting out triangles in the paper and taping over the triangles. Then use a utility knife to cut the edges so that you have a paper pattern of the room. Move the flooring sheet and the paper pattern to a larger room. Cut the flooring using the paper pattern.

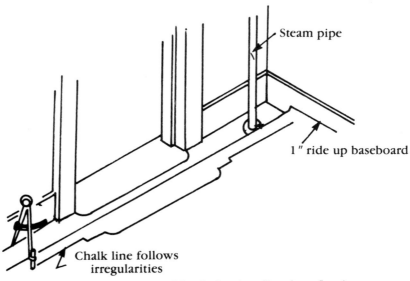

3-16   Scribing a wall line before installing sheet flooring.

To fit sheet flooring around a pipe (FIG. 3-17), measure the distance
(see A in the illustration) from the nearest end baseboard to the pipe and
transfer this distance to the flooring (**A**). Then measure (distance B) from
the pipe to the side baseboard and transfer this distance to the flooring
(**B**). Cut the pattern to the shape of the pipe where it enters the floor and
lay the pattern on the flooring in the correct place. Cut around the pattern
neatly. Cut a slip from the edge of the sheet to the hole so that the sheet
flooring can be fitted around the pipe. Move the flooring against the wall
and around the pipe to test the fit. Trim if necessary.

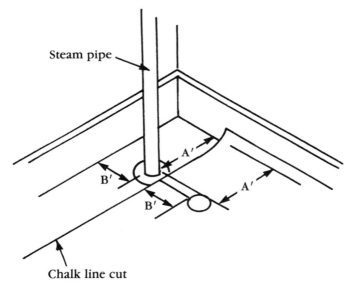

3-17 Fitting sheet flooring around a pipe.

Next, fit the ends of the sheet to the end baseboards. If the baseboard
is straight and even, draw a chalk line parallel to the end wall across the
flooring sheet, up the baseboard, and across the floor as shown in (FIG.
3-18). The line should be 1 to 2 feet from the end of the sheet. Measure the
distance (C) from the wall to the chalk line on the baseboard and transfer
the measurement to the flooring (C). Use a flexible metal tape rule for
accurate measurements on the sheet. Measure the distance (D) from the
wall to the chalked line on the floor and transfer to the flooring (D). Draw
a line between the two cutting marks and cut along the line.

To paste the flooring down, fold back one end of the sheet until it
meets the other end. Spread the mastic or adhesive on the exposed felt or
the subfloor. Replace the flooring over the adhesive on the exposed floor.
Repeat with the other end of the sheet.

To finish your sheet flooring job, cut the second piece 2 inches
longer than the room as described in FIG. 3-19. Lay the second piece over
the first piece with a 1-inch overlap. Set dividers so that the legs are 1/2

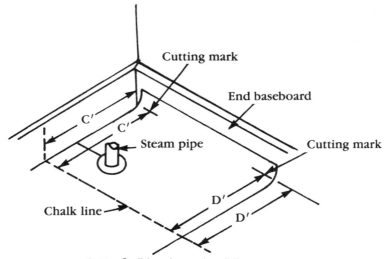

3-18 Scribing the end wall line.

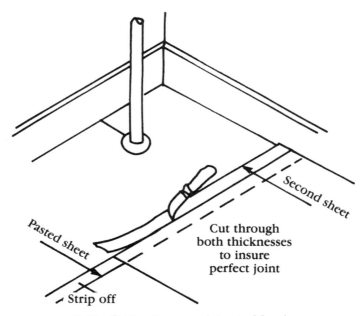

3-19 Cutting the second sheet of flooring.

inch apart. Set the sharp point at the edge of the second sheet and scribe a line the length of the sheet. Hold a linoleum knife at an exact right angle to the material and cut through the new sheet into the undersheet. Leave the guideline for the cut on the pasted sheet. Now cut along the line on the pasted sheet. Test the two new edges. They should butt exactly. Finally, paste the second sheet the same way as the first.

When the flooring is completely fitted and pasted, roll thoroughly with a flooring roller or rolling pin. Wait 24 hours, then wash thoroughly. Finally, replace the moldings. For most do-it-yourselfers, resilient tile floors are easier to install and trim than is larger sheet flooring.

Chapter **4**

Installing hard-tile floors

Tile has been used for hundreds of years because it is one of the most durable and easy to care for building materials. This practical tradition is being carried on today as the fashionable way to decorate your home—and not just in the kitchen or bath. Ceramic, mosaic, and quarry tiles are being installed throughout the home—in entryways, under woodstoves, and in hallways, bedrooms, kitchens, dining areas, dens, studies, and other rooms. Hard tiles offer a look of permanence.

Floor tiles can be laid on any solid surface as long as the base is firm and even. Exterior plywood laid over a subfloor forms an excellent base for a long-lasting tile floor. Exterior plywood is made with water-resistant glues; interior plywood is not. Floor tiles can also be laid over old linoleum or vinyl sheet flooring as long as the surface is clean, flat, and will accept the adhesive used.

INSTALLING CERAMIC MOSAIC TILE

A popular and easy type of floor tile to install is ceramic mosaic. It is a baked tile, is smaller in size than common tile, and is often manufactured in sheets held together by a fabric backing. This backing offers correct spacing for the grout, which is applied later. Let's take a look at the installation of this ceramic mosaic tile one step at a time.

Figure 4-1 illustrates how the sheets of ceramic mosaic tile are laid out on an older floor in order to decide on the correct spacing. The floor has been repaired as needed and checked for a smooth surface. If the floor were rough, it would have to be removed using techniques outlined in Chapter 3.

Once the ceramic mosaic sheets have been laid out, you must mark out a centerline for the room so that all sheets will be squared as they are installed. Find the centers of two sidewalls and draw a line between them using a straightedge (FIG. 4-2).

4-1 Ceramic-mosaic tile can be installed over prepared sheet flooring.

American Olean Tile Company

4-2 Drawing the line along which sheets of ceramic mosaic tile will be installed.

Make sure that the old floor has a good surface. Take off the old surface before applying the new tile surface.

If the old surface is rough, you will need to install a new smooth surface, called an underlayment, before you install the hard tile floor. A good choice for an underlayment is 3/16-inch Philippine mahogany plywood (FIG. 4-3). Make sure you place ring-shank nails every 6 to 10 inches to ensure that there will be no squeaks (FIG. 4-4).

The adhesive is prepared next. It should be smooth, trowelable, and lump-free. Don't mix more mortar than can be used in about 30 minutes because it will set up and be hard to use after that time.

4-3 A thin plywood underlayment provides a firm surface to which the new ceramic tile will adhere.

4-4 Underlayment must be tightly nailed with ring-shank nails to eliminate squeaks.

Next, apply the mortar. Spread the adhesive with a $1/8 \times 1/8 \times 1/8$-inch, notched trowel (FIG. 4-5) recommended for setting ceramic mosaics. Other adhesives will have other specifics. Use the flat edge of the trowel to lay down the mortar and the notched edge to smooth it out to the correct thickness.

4-5 Trowel for spreading ceramic mosaic tile mastic.

You're now ready to install the first sheet of ceramic mosaic tiles. Lay the sheet carefully. Make sure that the top edge matches the line drawn on the floor and the wall. Also make sure that there is not an excess or a lack of mortar under the tile sheets.

Once in place over the mortar, firmly seat the tile with a beating block. Make sure that the block is large enough to disperse pressure. Otherwise, a tile could be chipped or cracked, which would make it necessary for you to remove the sheet or make a repair to the individual tile. It's very important that you make sure all the tiles are carefully lined up, especially in a long room where a misaligned tile will break the floor's pattern.

Next comes the fun part: waiting. Depending on the type of adhesive used, you may have to wait 12 to 48 hours for the mortar to cure before you add the grout. Chapter 2 offers information and a table to guide you in the selection of ceramic mosaic tile grout.

Once the grout is mixed, it is spread over a small area on the surface of the ceramic mosaic tiles. This allows the grout to be worked into the space between the tiles and minimizing gaps and air spaces. The grout is spread with a rubber-faced grouting trowel designed especially for the job (FIG. 4-6). A hard metal trowel would scratch the surface of the tiles and not control the grout between convex-shaped tiles.

When you're done, sprinkle dry grout over the surface. Then rub the grouted surface of the tile with burlap to compact the joints and force out any trapped air.

Sometimes the surface you tile with ceramic tile is not flat. It may be stair-stepped or require a cove base. Figures 4-7 through 4-11 illustrate the installation of such tiles on stairs, at doorways, and on walls.

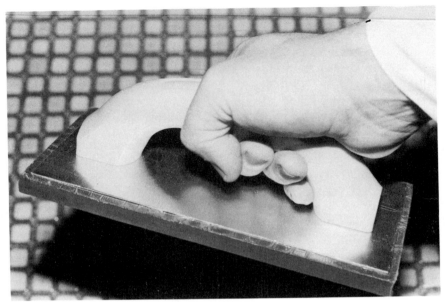

4-6   Rubber-faced grout trowel.

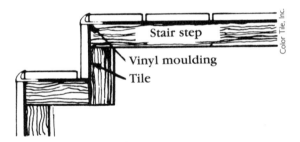

4-7   Installing tiles along stairs.

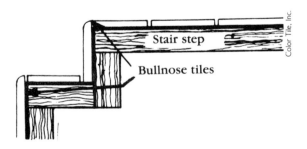

4-8   Using bullnose tiles on stairs.

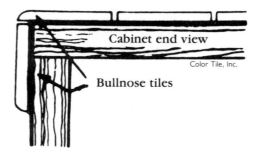

4-9 Installing bullnose tiles on the edge of a cabinet.

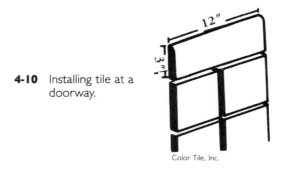

4-10 Installing tile at a doorway.

4-11 Installing a cove-base tile.

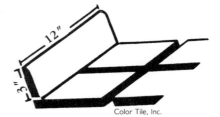

INSTALLING CERAMIC TILE

Ceramic tile is larger than ceramic mosaic and doesn't have the mesh bonding to evenly space the tiles, so it requires more skill to install. The following instructions, however, offer easy-to-follow steps for even the first-time do-it-yourselfer. The instructions specifically describe the installation of ceramic tile, but are equally valuable if you are laying quarry tile or paver floor.

The example shown in FIG. 4-12 was installed in a new greenhouse that was built onto a 50-year-old home made of granite rock. The ceramic tile was chosen both as a complementary decoration and as a practical heat sink to help collect and retain heat in the greenhouse. The existing patio was reinforced and then leveled with a 4-inch mortar bed.

The first step was to thoroughly clean the concrete slab. There are a variety of products available for this task through your tile retailer. If you are building over a wood subfloor, make sure that the surface is clean and flat. Refer to FIG. 4-13.

American Olean Tile Company

4-12 Newly added greenhouse anticipating the installation of a ceramic tile floor.

American Olean Tile Company

4-13 Beginning an installation with a thoroughly cleaned concrete slab.

To square off the room, draw lines across the width and length of the room to form a center point (FIG. 4-14). Parallel lines are then drawn as guide lines to ensure that the square tiles will be symmetrical with the square room.

Begin laying out the tile at the exterior edge of the greenhouse to where tiles will be installed. Any necessary cuts can then be made along the interior wall where they are less visible. Establish the starting lines by using two straightedges and a square edge (FIG. 4-15). Begin by establishing the position of the first three rows by placing a square edge against the line and against a straightedge, as shown in (FIG. 4-16).

4-14 Drawing guide lines.

American Olean Tile Company

4-15 Beginning at the exterior edge of the greenhouse floor.

American Olean Tile Company

4-16 Position the first three rows.

American Olean Tile Company

Every effort is made at the tile factories to ensure consistent color. The clay and the baking process, however, bring in variables that often make tiles slightly different in tint. To disperse the color variations throughout the floor and make a more beautiful design, shuffle the tiles before installation (FIG. 4-17). Select tile from three boxes, make sure the batch number is the same, and shuffle the tile for a thorough mix.

The next step is to mix the adhesive mortar (FIG. 4-18). There are various mortars and floor mixes available. Use the one recommended for your specific type of tile and installation factors. The sample mix includes latex additives to accommodate expansion and contraction.

Using the smooth side of a $1/4 \times 3/8 \times 1/4$-inch notched trowel, spread the floor mix in a small area (FIG. 4-19). Comb the mortar with the notched edge of the trowel to ensure an even distribution. Install a row of tile against the straightedge, which has been placed along the guide lines. Many do-it-yourselfers purchase and use spacers (FIG. 4-20) to make sure that the tiles are evenly spaced.

Once the first row is in, set additional rows by lining up the joints (FIG. 4-21). After the first three rows are laid, use a wood block to beat the tile flat into the mortar to ensure a good bond (FIG. 4-22).

Periodically remove one tile to check the bond (FIG. 4-23). Mortar must evenly cover the back of the tile and bond with the concrete slab. This is crucial, especially in a passive solar design, because air pockets will not permit efficient conduction of the Sun's heat through to the mortar bed for storage.

4-17 Shuffle tiles before installation.

American Olean Tile Company

4-18 Mix the adhesive mortar.

American Olean Tile Company

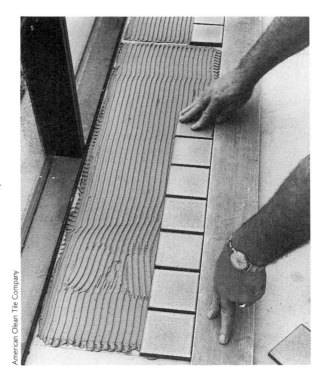

4-19 Spread the floor mix in a small area.

American Olean Tile Company

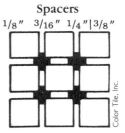

Spacers

1/8″ 3/16″ 1/4″|3/8″

4-20 Installing spacers between tiles.

Color Tile, Inc.

The next section of tile is set in a similar manner. Use the straightedge for the sixth row and filling in the next two rows. Check frequently with the square edge to be sure joints are lined up (FIG. 4-24).

Partial tiles have to be installed (FIG. 4-25) when you reach an inside wall. Cuts are made with a tile cutter (FIG. 4-26), as explained in Chapter 2. Sometimes a special cut must be made in a tile to fit around an obstacle, such as a rock in a wall (FIG. 4-27). This cut is made with tile nippers.

Finally, the floor tiles are set (FIG. 4-28). Depending on the mortar used and local weather conditions, you should wait 3 or 4 days to allow the flooring to cure before grout is installed. Grouting too soon could cause the tile to shift and make repairs difficult.

American Olean Tile Company

4-21 Spacing between tiles can also be done with a straightedge and your eyes.

American Olean Tile Company

4-22 Beat the tile with a wooden block to ensure a good bond.

4-23 Remove one tile to check bond.

4-24 Set the next section of tile.

American Olean Tile Company

4-25 Installing partial tiles along the inside wall.

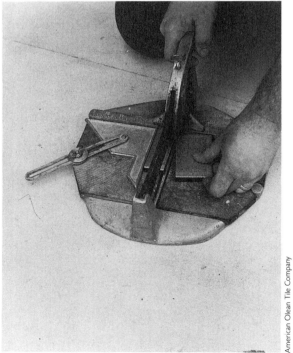

American Olean Tile Company

4-26 Using a tile cutter to snap the scored tile.

American Olean Tile Company

4-27 Special cut-to-fit rough outline on rock wall.

Grout should be selected based upon the type of tile, the type of installation, and the manufacturer's and dealer's recommendations. The grout should be mixed thoroughly (FIG. 4-29). Check to see that there is no powder at the bottom. Scrape off the sides of the bucket. The grout should be the consistency of marshmallow fluff. Let it set for a few minutes, then remix.

Once the tile has set and you are sure it won't shift when it is walked on, mix the grout and spread it on (FIG. 4-30). Use a rubber-faced grouting trowel to spread the grout so that it fills the joints between the tiles. When you're done, scrape the excess grout away along the edges (FIGS. 4-31 and 4-32) with a putty knife.

Next, sprinkle dry grout mix over the tile surface to absorb moisture in the joints until the joints appear dark and moist (FIG. 4-33). Use a clean, dry cloth to rub the tile surface in a circular motion to loosen excess grout and to compact the joints (FIG. 4-34). Allow the floor to stand for at least 15 minutes.

Use a damp Turkish towel to wipe the tile surface clean of excess grout (FIG. 4-35). Rinse the towel and change the water frequently (FIG. 4-36). Continue wiping until the tile appears clean (FIG. 4-37). A slight film will develop on the tile as the floor dries.

It's time to step back and take a look (FIG. 4-38). Notice the even shading of the tile and the flat, compact joints in the grouted floor.

4-28 Tile floor is set. Wait three or four days for curing.

High-traffic entryways benefit from resilient tile floors.

Floor patterns can bring spring indoors.

Resilient tile flooring can simulate ceramic tile flooring.

Resilient tile flooring can simulate hardwood flooring.

Flooring colors can
reflect room colors.

Flooring colors can also
contrast room colors.

Resilient flooring can
simulate slate flooring.

Large patterns are best
used in larger rooms.

4-29 Mix grout thoroughly.

American Olean Tile Company

4-30 Spreading grout with a grout trowel.

American Olean Tile Company

American Olean Tile Company

4-31 Scrape excess grout from the edge.

American Olean Tile Company

4-32 Removing grout from entryway.

4-33 Sprinkle dry grout over the tile surface.

American Olean Tile Company

4-34 Rub the tile to loosen excess grout and compact joints.

American Olean Tile Company

American Olean Tile Company

4-35 Wipe tile surface with damp towel.

American Olean Tile Company

4-36 Rinse towel and change water frequently.

4-37 Repeat wiping until the tile appears clean.

American Olean Tile Company

4-38 Inspecting the cleaned tile floor.

American Olean Tile Company

Again, you should give your new floor a few days to dry out before you clean up. A final cleanup can be done using a concrete and masonry cleaner (FIG. 4-39). This cleaner contains acids, stains, and mortar deposits.

Scrub the tile surface briskly with a brush and the solution (FIG. 4-40). This cleaner will not stain metal and may be applied to a dry floor. Use a long-handled brush to keep splatters away from your skin. Rubber gloves are also recommended. Allow the solution to stand on the tile for 7 to 8 minutes for best results.

Finally, use a large sponge to flood the area with clean water (FIG. 4-41). Then drag a towel through the puddles to lift off the solution and grout (FIG. 4-42). Squeeze the saturated towel into a bucket. Repeat the process for the final rinse (FIG. 4-43). Flood the floor with clear water again and wipe dry. Continue dragging the towel and wringing it dry until all water is removed from the floor. The tile should now be clean and sparkling with no trace of grout or streaks (FIG. 4-44).

Figure 4-45 illustrates how the new ceramic tile floor blends in with the rest of the house. The living room extends under the Sun. Ceramic tile warms the floor of this passive-solar, glass-enclosed porch by conducting the Sun's heat into the cement slab below. Shady leaves from the backyard tree keep it cool in the summer. Screen windows and door add ventilation. The sunroom also opens to an outdoor patio.

Sometimes a floor will extend on to a nearby wall with tile making the transition. This is especially popular in the bathroom where a ceramic tile floor blends into a ceramic tile shower. Figures 4-46 through 4-50 illustrate how this can be easily accomplished by the do-it-yourselfer.

4-39 Concrete and masonry cleaner.

American Olean Tile Company

4-40 Scrub the tile surface briskly with brush and solution.

American Olean Tile Company

4-41 Flood the area with clean water using a large sponge.

American Olean Tile Company

American Olean Tile Company

4-42 Drag a towel through the puddles to lift off the solution and grout.

American Olean Tile Company

4-43 Repeat the process for the final rinse.

4-44 A cleaned and sparkling tile floor.

American Olean Tile Company

4-45 The finished greenhouse room.

American Olean Tile Company

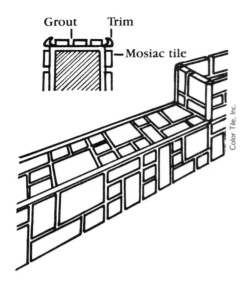

4-46 Installing mosaic tile on the shower sill and jamb.

Mosiac tile with vinyl trim

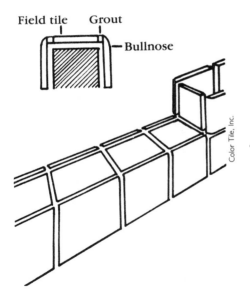

4-47 Installing ceramic tile on the shower sill and jamb.

Method one—when your door opening jamb and sill is 4¹/₄ " or less, you can use 4¹/₄ " field tile on the jamb and sill of the door opening and 4¹/₄ " bullnose on the facing on either side.

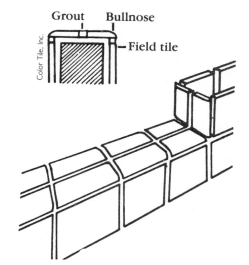

4-48 An alternate method of installing ceramic tile on the shower sill and jamb.

Method two—when your door jamb and sill is larger than 4 1/2 ", you can use two 4 1/4 " bullnose pieces cut to size on the jamb and sill of the door opening with a grout joint in the center. You then use regular field tile on the facing on either side.

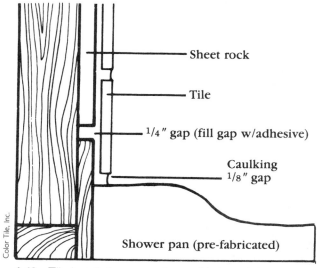

4-49 Tile installation around a prefabricated shower pan.

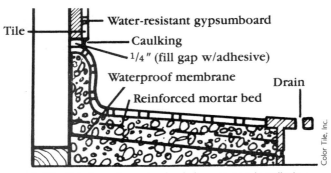

4-50 Reinforced mortar-bed shower pan installation.

INSTALLING QUARRY TILE

Quarry tile can add the perfect touch of sophistication to your home and adds a lifetime floor covering to any room. Its durable composition can handle heavy traffic areas.

Preparation and installation techniques are, for the most part, very similar to those for other types of ceramic tile. Refer to earlier illustrated steps for how to install quarry tile.

First, prepare the subfloor surface as you would for ceramic tile according to the type of adhesive you will be using and the manufacturer's directions for that adhesive. Next, establish working lines as you would for ceramic tile.

Most of the tools and supplies used for ceramic tile installation can be used for quarry tile installation as well—trowels, cutters, nippers, spacers, etc. Assemble all tools and supplies. Make sure all the cartons of tiles are uniform and that the tiles are in acceptable condition.

To set quarry tile, first mix the adhesive according to the manufacturer's directions. Apply the adhesive to the subfloor with a notched trowel. Work only one quadrant at a time.

Next, set all whole tiles, using the pyramid sequence described earlier. Quarry tiles generally have wider joints than ceramic tiles. To achieve a wider, even joint, you can do one of two things: add spacers between each tile to achieve uniform spacing or use a line gauge that automatically measures and establishes spacing between quarry tiles. Make sure all lines and joints are straight and uniform. Then remove excess adhesive from the tile while the adhesive is still wet.

Set the remaining quadrants in the same manner. Then measure and cut quarry border tiles as you would ceramic border tiles. Allow the adhesive to dry 24 hours before applying grout.

For unglazed quarry tile, use a recommended grout release. Mix the grout according to the manufacturer's directions, then apply the grout to the tile surface with a rubber-faced trowel. Work thoroughly into joints. Sponge excess grout off the tiles with a damp sponge.

Remove the film by buffing with a dry, soft cleaning pad. Caulk and seal the grouted surface after the grout is completely cured, which usually takes from 72 hours to 2 weeks. Buff the sealed surface with a clean rag.

INSTALLING WALL MOLDINGS

Once your hard-tile floor is finished, you can add the wood trim, or molding, around the circumference of the room. Base molding serves as a border between the finished floor and the wall. It is available in several widths and forms. Two-piece base consists of a baseboard topped with a small base cap (FIG. 4-51). When the wall is not straight and true, the small base molding will conform more closely to the variations than will the wider one. A common size for this type of baseboard is $5/8 \times 31/4$ inches or wider (FIG. 4-52). Although a wood trim is desirable at the junction of the wall and floor because it serves as a protective bumper, wood trim is sometimes eliminated entirely. Most baseboards are finished with a base shoe, which is usually $1/2 \times 1/4$ inch in size, as shown in FIGS. 4-51 and 4-52.

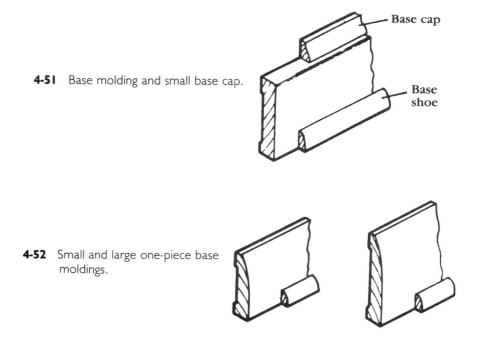

4-51   Base molding and small base cap.

Base cap

Base shoe

4-52   Small and large one-piece base moldings.

Square-edge baseboards should be installed with a butt joint at the inside corners (FIG. 4-53) and a mitered joint at the outside corners (FIG. 4-54). It should be nailed to each stud with two 8d (eight-penny) finishing nails. Molded, single-piece bases, base moldings, and base shoes have a coped joint at the inside corners and a mitered joint at the outside corners. A coped joint is one in which the first piece is square-cut against the wall or base, and the second molding coped. This is done by sawing a 45-degree miter cut and then, with a coping saw, trimming the molding along the inner line of the miter (FIG. 4-54).

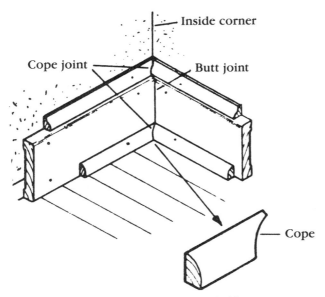

4-53 Butt joint base molding at inside corner

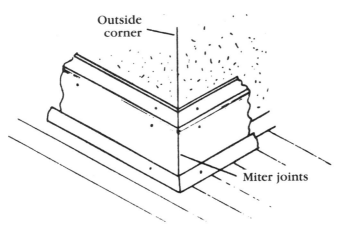

4-54 Miter joint base molding at outside corner.

The base shoe should be nailed to the flooring with long, slender nails, not to the baseboard itself. Thus, if the joists shrink a small amount, no opening will occur under the shoe.

Chapter **5**

Maintaining tile floors

*P*roper care and protection will keep your resilient or hard-tile floor looking beautiful and performing at its best. Just how much attention it needs will depend on the type of floor you buy and on how much traffic it gets every day.

All floor covering needs to be washed on a regular basis to keep it clean and presentable. Floor washing techniques will be covered later. Keeping your floor looking its best also requires preventive care to avoid gouges, stains, scratches, chips, etc.

CARING FOR RESILIENT FLOORS

Only a few minutes of daily care can go a long way toward helping your resilient floor look its best. Here are a few tips to help you decide what to do and when.

If you've just installed a new vinyl floor, damp mop it immediately. Don't scrub or wash your new floor, though, for at least another 5 days.

When moving heavy furniture or appliances, use plywood or hardboard panels and walk the furniture or appliance across the panel. Another way is to slip a scrap of carpet or rug face down under each leg and slide the furniture carefully to avoid scratching or gouging. Be careful, however, some carpet dyes can walk off and permanently stain resilient flooring. Ask your flooring retailer about the color fastness of your carpeting.

Asphalt compounds, like driveway sealers, can also permanently stain resilient flooring. Place mats or throw rugs near outside doors to keep asphalt, dirt, and moisture from being tracked onto the floor. Some rubber-backed mats also can cause the floor to discolor in time. It's best to use a mat or rug that doesn't have a rubber or latex backing.

Sweep, dust-mop, or vacuum your floor daily to remove loose dirt before it can scratch your floor's surface. Wipe up wet spills before they dry. Remove dried spills with a damp cloth or mop.

Use floor protectors on the legs of furniture to minimize scratches and indentations. Floor protectors are available from your flooring retailer and at most hardware stores.

Roller-type casters on furniture may damage resilient flooring. Be certain that caster wheels or glides have a flat surface contact with your floor. If not, change them or place floor protectors under them.

CARING FOR NO-WAX FLOORS

No-wax floor tiles have become popular in the home furnishings market in the last few years because they do not need to be scrubbed and/or waxed. The no-wax tiles have a special wear and gloss layer that shines without waxing.

No-wax doesn't mean no care, however. Although the new no-wax floors are bright, shiny, and easier to clean than regular vinyl floor tiles, they still require cleaning. This is true of any surface in the home, especially one that takes the abuse and pounding that a floor receives. Here are some suggestions that will help you maintain the sparkling appearance of your no-wax tile floors (FIGS. 5-1 and 5-2).

Sweep or vacuum your floor to remove loose dirt. Floors that are lightly soiled should be mopped or sponged with clean water to help remove the dirt. Since no-wax tile surfaces tend to hide dirt, the floor should be washed regularly with a mild household detergent. Don't use soap-based cleaners because they can leave a dulling film.

Use a mop or sponge to apply the detergent to a small area of the floor. Pressure on the mop or sponge should be enough to clean the embossed design on the tile surface. For stubborn dirt, use the nylon cleaning pad on the mop. Don't use abrasive pads such as steel wool or scouring pads. Rinse the floor thoroughly with clean warm water to prevent dirty water from remaining on the embossed areas. Remember, no-wax tile floors do not require buffing.

Azrock Floor Products

5-1 No-wax tile floors can be maintained with a minimum of effort.

5-2   Today's tile floors can keep a sheen much longer than waxed linoleum.

Azrock Floor Products

In areas that are used constantly, heavy foot traffic could begin to reduce some of the surface gloss on a no-wax floor. To restore luster, use a no-wax floor finish after you clean the floor and allow it to completely dry. If you decide to apply a second coat of floor finish, do so after the first is completely dry.

No-wax floors can be damaged by intense heat and lighted cigarettes, as well as rubber- or foam-backed mats or rugs. Avoid applying carnauba or water waxes and vinyl dressings because they will not adhere. They will create a dull film, or haze, on your floor, however.

Commonly used household products can stain your no-wax floor and should be wiped up immediately with an absorbent paper towel or cloth. The floor should then be washed with a full-strength detergent. If this doesn't remove the stain, try rubbing it with alcohol or lighter fluid. Spills from certain products can be cleaned by following the instructions below.

Iodine, mustard, mercurochrome, merthiolate, and certain ink spills should be wiped up with an absorbent paper towel or cloth. Remove the stain by dampening a clean cloth with rubbing alcohol and wiping the surface area. Wait 30 minutes before walking on the area.

Asphalt, inks, shoe polish, and tar stains can be removed by rubbing a cloth dampened with lighter fluid over the stained areas.

Remove paint stains and varnishes by wiping a cloth dampened with turpentine or paint thinner over the spill. Never use paint remover on a no-wax floor tile.

CARING FOR VINYL FLOORS

Resilient vinyl floor tile requires more care than no-wax flooring, but can be easy to maintain (FIGS. 5-3 and 5-4).

Wash the floor with a general-purpose liquid detergent made according to the label instructions. Ideally, you should use one sponge mop and bucket to wash the floor and another mop and bucket to rinse it. If you use only one mop, no matter how much you wring it out, you won't get all the detergent out of the sponge and a dulling film will be left on your floor.

Dip your sponge mop into the cleaning solution, and without wringing it out, spread the cleaning solution on a small area of the floor—about 3 × 3 feet. Relax for a minute and let the cleaning solution do the work for you. The detergent action will loosen a lot of the dirt and keep it suspended for easy pickup.

Now go over the area again with the sponge mop, this time scrubbing hard enough to loosen the remaining dirt. If you have a mop with a nylon scrubbing pad, you can get up hard-to-remove marks with the nylon pad.

Wring out the sponge mop thoroughly to take up the cleaning solution left on the floor. With a second bucket of clean warm water and a rinse-only mop, rinse the floor thoroughly. Often, general-purpose detergent directions will say rinsing is not necessary. While this may be true on other surfaces, it's not true on floors. Any detergent film left on a floor will hold tracked-in dirt and dull the surface.

5-3   A resilient vinyl-composition tile floor.

5-4 Vinyl tile is often used in high-traffic businesses due to ease of maintenance.

Repeat this procedure of washing and rinsing one area at a time until the whole floor is clean. Change rinse water often to make sure you're not redepositng any dirt or detergent. Allow the floor to dry thoroughly before walking on it. If you intend to apply a protective floor polish the same day, make sure your floor is completely dry before applying the polish.

A word of caution: never use steel wool or scouring cleaners on vinyl floor tile. For heavily soiled or exceptionally dirty areas, thoroughly clean with a full-strength cleaner designed for your specific floor. Allow the cleaner to soak in a few minutes, then use a nylon pad or scrub brush to loosen the dirt.

APPLYING FLOOR POLISH

Here's how to apply floor polish to your vinyl or similar tile floor. First, wash the floor thoroughly. Then allow the floor to dry at least 20 to 30 minutes.

Apply the polish in a thin, uniform coat. Do not use a sponge mop that has been used previously to clean the floor. There will always be some detergent film in the sponge, which can cause the polish to streak and cloud.

To apply a thin coat, pour the floor polish directly onto the applicator. Or, put the polish in a bucket, then dip in the mop, and wring it out gently. When applying polish, move the applicator in all directions to ensure even distribution. Don't rub the applicator too vigorously, since this can cause bubbles.

When multiple coats of polish are to be applied, wait at least 30 minutes between each application. Make sure you follow specific drying instructions on the polish container. Allow the polish to dry completely before using the room.

REMOVING FLOOR POLISH

Stripping polish removes the successive layers of polish and dirt. The best way to tell whether your floor needs to be stripped is to test-strip a small, out-of-the-way area. Compare the results against the surrounding area. If the rest of the floor has noticeably less pattern and color clarity, chances are that stripping and repolishing are needed.

First, sweep or vacuum the floor thoroughly. Apply a liberal amount of a good wax or polish remover over a 3 × 3-foot area with a sponge mop. Allow the solution to stand 3 to 5 minutes so it can soak in and soften the polish.

Next, use a sponge mop, nonwoven pad, scrub brush, or electrical floor scrubber with nonabrasive pads to loosen the old polish film. Pick up the cleaning solution and old polish with a sponge mop or cloth. Rinse the floor with warm water and a clean sponge mop. If some film remains from the old polish, repeat the stripping operation where needed, then rinse.

Repeat the procedure area by area until the entire floor is stripped. Let the floor dry. It should look dull but clean and is now ready for polishing, as outlined above.

CARING FOR LINOLEUM

While most resilient floors installed today are vinyl or no-wax, there are still many thousands of homes that have long-lasting linoleum flooring. Specific instructions on how to maintain linoleum flooring follow.

Linoleum, whether on floors, kitchen countertops, walls, or other inside surfaces, will stay attractive longer and wear better if it is waxed and polished. A few simple rules for its care are useful:

1. Dust daily.
2. Use water sparingly.
3. Clean with special mild linoleum cleaner, soap, or mild detergent solution.
4. Apply wax in a thin, even film.
5. Rewax only as needed, usually no more than once a month.
6. Never use harsh abrasives other than fine steel wool to take off spots that are hard to remove.

No matter what type of wax is used, always start with a clean surface. There are some excellent linoleum cleaners that may be diluted with water in accordance with the manufacturer's directions. When using a cleaner, clean only a few square feet at a time, go over the area with a fresh cloth that has been rinsed and wrung out with clear, lukewarm water. Permit the surface to dry thoroughly so that the wax will spread evenly.

Waxes that protect linoleum are essentially of two types: paste and liquid waxes with a volatile-solvent base, and self-polishing waxes with a water-emulsion base. They should be applied in very thin coats to avoid making the floor slippery.

Volatile-solvent waxes may be obtained in either paste or liquid form. The liquid is somewhat easier to apply than the paste because of the large proportion of solvent. Both paste and liquid are suitable for linoleum, as well as for other types of floor surfaces.

Paste wax should be applied with a slightly dampened soft cloth or with a wax applicator. It should be allowed to dry and then polished to a lustrous finish. Liquid wax should be spread evenly over the cleaned surface with a lamb's wool applicator in straight, parallel strokes. After drying for 30 minutes, it should be polished to a lustrous finish. Waxes of the organic-solvent type must not be used on asphalt tile because they soften and mar the surface of the tile.

Self-polishing or water-emulsion base waxes will give a protective coating if used on linoleum, rubber tile, cork, asphalt tile, mastic, and other flooring. The wax should be spread as thinly and evenly as possible with a lamb's wool applicator or soft cloth mop in straight, parallel strokes. If properly applied, it should dry to a hard, lustrous film in less than 30 minutes. Although not required, the gloss may be increased by a slight buffing after the wax is thoroughly dry.

A weighted floor brush or electric polishing machine does an efficient job with little effort. A floor polisher may be rented at a variety of retail outlets or rental yards. For a very hard surface, the linoleum should be given two or three coats of wax. Make sure each coat dries for at least 30 minutes before it is polished.

Care should be taken not to flood linoleum surfaces with water. Any water that seeps through the edges or seams may affect the cementing material and cause the backing to mildew or rot and edges of the linoleum to become loose and curled. Wipe up water as soon as it is spilled on waxed linoleum to keep light spots from appearing. Grease and other spots should be cleaned as quickly as possible with a cloth or sponge wrung out of mild lukewarm detergent solution. Rinse by using a clean cloth wrung out of clear, lukewarm water. Floor oils and sweeping compounds containing oils should not be used on linoleum because these materials may leave a film of oil on the surface, which will collect dust and dirt.

CARING FOR ASPHALT TILE

Another flooring product commonly found in older homes is asphalt tile. Asphalt tile is often used to cover concrete and wood floors and is found in a variety of colors. Impervious to water, the tiles are especially suitable for floors on which water is likely to be spilled, such as kitchens, laundries, and bathrooms. Asphalt tile also provides attractive and satisfactory flooring for basement recreation rooms and enclosed porches.

Mastic floor covering of the asphalt type has asphalt, bitumen, or resin as the base and often lasts many years. Cleansers and polishes containing abrasives, oils, or organic solvents (gasoline, turpentine, carbon tetrachloride) should not be used to clean asphalt-base coverings, however. Never use unknown cleaning preparations on asphalt tile without testing them first, unless they are recommended by the manufacturer of the flooring.

To test a cleaning or polishing preparation before using it on asphalt tile, moisten a white cloth with the preparation and rub over the surface of a spare tile. If the color of the tile shows on the cloth, the preparation has acted as a solvent and dissolved the surface of the tile. It is not safe to use.

Asphalt tile floors may be washed with neutral soap and lukewarm water in much the same manner as linoleum. The water will not harm the tile unless it is permitted to stand and seep under the edges enough to loosen them from the floor. After they are cleaned and dried, the care of asphalt tile floors is similar to that recommended for linoleum with one very important exception. Never use paste wax or liquid wax that has a solvent base on asphalt tiles. These waxes will soften the tile and mar the surface.

Water-emulsion or self-polishing waxes that are free from oils are suitable and safe for asphalt tile. They should be spread as thinly as possible on the surface of the floor with a lamb's-wool applicator. Use straight, parallel strokes in one direction only. In approximately 30 minutes, the wax should dry to a hard, lustrous finish. While these waxes are self-polishing to a degree, the appearance of the floor will be improved by a light buffing. Before you polish, however, the wax should be completely dry.

Wax should be renewed at intervals, depending on the severity of wear. It is not necessary to rewax as long as the floor responds to polishing. Daily dusting and occasional machine polishing will eliminate the need for mopping and extend the life of the wax coating.

CARING FOR CERAMIC TILE

Ceramic floor and wall tile is extremely easy to care for (FIGS. 5-5 through 5-7). In most cases, simply wiping the tile with a wet cloth will remove dirt and grime. More specifically, let's look at the methods of cleaning glazed tiles, ceramic mosaics, and quarry tiles.

Glazed tiles in bathrooms and other areas are easy to routinely clean. If you have soft water, use an all-purpose cleaner on the tiles. Allow it to stand for about 5 minutes before lightly scrubbing the tile with a sponge. Rinse well. If you have hard water, commercial tile cleaners, which are available at supermarkets, will do the best job. As an alternate, a solution of white vinegar and water in equal amounts should remove deposits. Test this method in a small area first to be sure the vinegar doesn't etch your tile or erode your grout. Vinegar can damage some crystalline tile glazes.

For a heavy-duty cleaning of ceramic floor and wall tile, an all-purpose cleaner should be used in areas where dirt is likely to build up. The cleaner should be applied and allowed to stand for about 5 minutes before the tile is scrubbed lightly with a brush. Hard water deposits can be removed with a commercial tile cleaner or treated with a solution of equal amounts white vinegar and water.

Cleaning ceramic mosaic tile floors is similar. For routine cleaning, wipe with a damp sponge mop. You can supplement with a diluted solution of a popular household cleaner. For heavy-duty cleaning, mix a household scouring powder with water until it makes a pastelike consistency and then mop it over the floors. Allow the paste to stand for about 5 minutes. Scrub vigorously with a scrubbing brush. Rinse and wipe dry. It should be noted, however, that as ceramic mosaic floor tiles age, a patina forms on the surface. Its soft shine keeps the floor looking fresh longer and makes maintenance easier.

Here are some notes on maintaining quarry tile floors. For routine cleaning, mop occasionally with any popular household cleaner. Rinse thoroughly to keep dull detergent film from drying on the tile surface. For heavy-duty cleaning, a thorough scrubbing with an all-purpose cleaner or scouring powder paste is recommended. Scrub vigorously with a more concentrated cleaner solution. Rinse completely. Use scouring powder for any stubborn spots that remain. Quarry tiles, too, need less maintenance as they age.

5-5 The care of entryway tile floors is especially important.

Tile Council of America

5-6 Ceramic mosaic tile offer a hard surface that can be shined easily.

5-7 Quarry tile was selected for beauty and ease of maintenance in this community center.

REMOVING STAINS FROM HARD TILE

Here are some guidelines for removing stains from ceramic tile and grout.

- **Blood** Use hydrogen peroxide or household bleach.
- **Coffee, tea, food, fruit juices, and lipstick** Use popular household cleansers mixed with hot water followed by hydrogen peroxide or household bleach. Rinse and dry.
- **Fingernail polish** Dissolve with polish remover. If stains remain, apply liquid household bleach. Rinse and dry.
- **Grease and fats** Use soda and water or Spic & Span (or equivalent) and warm water.
- **Inks and colored dyes** Apply household bleach. Let stand until the stain disappears, keeping the surface wet. Rinse and dry.
- **Iodine** Scrub with ammonia. Rinse and dry.
- **Mercurochrome** USe liquid household bleach.
- **Mildew** Use X-14 Instant Mildew Stain Remover (or equivalent) for tile and grout, or scrub tile with ammonia, and scrub grout with a scouring powder. Wash with a bleach if needed. Rinse and dry.

Be sure to refer to the tile manufacturer's literature before cleaning or removing stains from resilient or hard tile. The manufacturer will make recommendations based on laboratory tests and customer comments. Some will even make specific product and brand name recommendations.

Chapter **6**

Repairing tile floors

Repairing resilient and hard-tile floor coverings is actually much easier than most do-it-yourselfers realize. Defective tiles can be lifted out and replaced with new tiles. In this chapter, you'll learn how to make repairs to resilient and hard-tile floors, as well as to the subflooring below them.

Hopefully, your floor doesn't look like the one in FIG. 6-1. Even if it does, however, your flooring can be renewed or replaced. You should plan to execute all other interior repairs before beginning the repair of your floor. If you plan on saving the flooring material, cover it. Otherwise, ignore it as you make other repairs.

REPAIRING SELF-ADHERING TILE

There are numerous brands of self-adhering resilient tile on the market. The principles of installation and replacement for all types are the same.

6-1 Hopefully, your floor doesn't look like this one.

Once you've decided that a specific tile should be replaced, identify the problem and decide how many tiles will need to be replaced. Hopefully, you have some extra tiles in the garage or up on a closet shelf for just such an emergency. By checking the unused tiles, you can decide whether or not it is a self-adhering type.

When you remove the old tile, be sure that you don't damage the adjacent tiles. One way of avoiding this is by cutting the defective tile in half and pulling it out from the center rather than the edges.

Once the defective, self-adhering tile is removed, the subfloor should be checked for smoothness. It may possibly be the reason why the tile was damaged. It may be that a subfloor nail has popped up or that there was a rock or other object under the tile when it was laid. In any case, make sure that the replacement tile will not be damaged in the same manner.

After the defective tile has been removed and the area cleaned, lay the new tile in place with the adhesive cover still on. This way, you can match the size and color of the tile and surrounding tiles before you install them. Some linoleum and vinyl tiles will have faded in color. You may be able to use common household bleach to match colors, or a thorough cleaning of the surrounding tile may rejuvenate the colors. Newer vinyl and better-quality no-wax flooring probably will not have faded and may only need a thorough cleaning (see Chapter 5).

Finally, strip off the backing paper and install the new self-adhering tile (FIG. 6-2). You may then want to place a heavy object, such as a block, on the surface to assist the bonding. Make sure that the object will not mar the surface of the new tile. Depending upon the type of flooring, you may now want to wax or polish the floor, especially around the new tile.

6-2 Installing replacement, self-adhering tile.

REPAIRING RESILIENT TILE

The majority of the resilient tile floors installed in new and older homes are not self-adhering. Instead, they are installed using a mastic or adhesive, as outlined in Chapter 3. So what do you do if tiles have come loose from the subfloor, are damaged and need to be replaced (FIG. 6-3) and you want to do the job yourself?

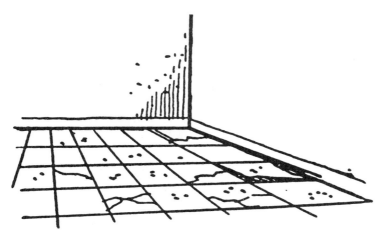

6-3   A tile floor with loose and damaged tile.

First, you'll need some tools and supplies (FIG. 6-4), including a container to mix in, adhesive for the kind of tile you have, a paintbrush or putty knife, a knife or saw, and the number of new tiles needed. If you don't have any leftover tile, check with the retailer from which you purchased the original tile. If you didn't install it, take a tile to any large tile retailer in the area for help with a match.

The first step when replacing resilient tile is to remove any loose or damaged tiles. A warm iron will help soften the adhesive (FIG. 6-5). Scrape the old adhesive off the floor (FIG. 6-6). Also, scrape the old adhesive off the back of the old tile if you are going to use it again.

Next, carefully fit the tiles together on the floor. Some tile can be cut with a knife (FIG. 6-7) or shares; others with a saw. Tile is less apt to break if it is warm.

Lift up the tiles and spread the adhesive on the floor with a paint brush (FIG. 6-8) or putty knife, depending upon the consistency of the adhesive. Wait until the adhesive begins to set before you place the tile. Press the tile firmly into place and roll over it with a rolling pin (FIG. 6-9).

It's that easy. You've repaired your resilient tile floor and saved money, too.

REPAIRING CERAMIC TILE

The replacement or repair of ceramic tile is also easy to accomplish. The first step is to scrape off the old adhesive from the floor (FIG. 6-10). You can also scrape the adhesive from the old tile if you plan to reuse it.

6-4 Tools and supplies you need to repair a tile floor.

6-5 Using a warm iron to soften the adhesive on the back of a floor tile.

6-6 Scrape off the old adhesive.

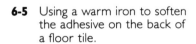

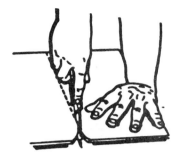

6-7 Cut tile with a knife or household shears.

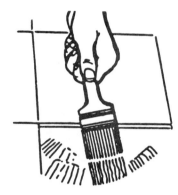

6-8 Spread adhesive on the floor with a paint brush or putty knife.

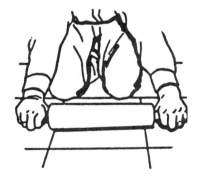

6-9 Press the tile firmly with a rolling pin.

6-10 Scrape old adhesive from the floor before replacing ceramic tile.

If you are using new tile and need to fit it, mark it carefully to size. You can then score it with a tile cutter or a glass cutter. It should then snap off if you press it on the edge of a hard surface (FIG. 6-11).

6-11   Snapping a scored ceramic tile.

Spread the adhesive on the floor and on the back of the tile. Press the tile firmly into place (FIG. 6-12).

Joints on ceramic tile should be filled with grout after the tile has set. Mix powdered grout with water to form a stiff paste. Then press the mixture into the joints with your fingers (FIG. 6-13). Smooth the surface. Carefully remove excess grout from the tile surface before it dries (FIG. 6-14).

6-12   Press the floor tile into place.

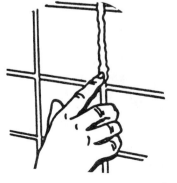

6-13   Press the grout mixture between the tiles.

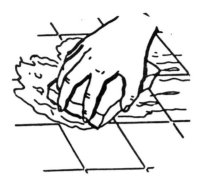

6-14 Remove excess grout before it dries.

Dispose of the excess grout mixture in a trash container—not down the drain. Then clean up the surfaces and tools (FIG. 6-15). Allow the grout to dry before you use the floor.

The job is complete and your ceramic tile floor is repaired. The same techniques can be used to repair ceramic wall tiles.

6-15 Clean up tools and containers.

REPAIRING SUBFLOORS

The floors in most homes are composed of two separate layers. The bottom layer is called the subfloor and is made of rough, tongue-and groove lumber that is nailed directly to the floor joists. In some cases, this subfloor will run diagonally to the joists, while in others it will run at right angles to them. A layer of building paper often covers the subfloor to keep out dust and dirt. Then, the finish flooring is placed at right angles to the subfloor.

Here are a variety of maladies that occur in the subfloor and affect the finish flooring itself. One of the most common is the creaking floor symptom. In most cases, a creaking floor is caused when the nails that hold the subfloor to the joists loosen. They may either pull loose or be loosened when the wood shrinks.

If the creak is in the subfloor and the underside is exposed, as when the flooring functions as the ceiling for an unfinished basement, drive a small wedge between the joist and the loose board (FIG. 6-16). It will take up the play in the board and the noise will stop. If several boards are loose, nail a piece of wood to the joist at a level high enough to prevent these boards from moving down (FIG. 6-17). The nailheads will keep the boards from moving up and effectively end the noise.

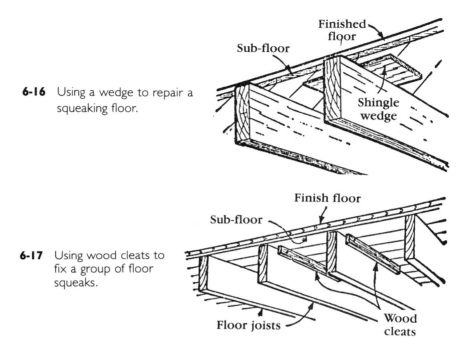

6-16 Using a wedge to repair a squeaking floor.

6-17 Using wood cleats to fix a group of floor squeaks.

In many cases, it is impossible to reach the subfloor without tearing up the finish floor or removing a ceiling. As neither of these is feasible, the only alternative is to try to locate the floor joist by tapping on the floor. If a floor joist near the creak is located, then 2- or 3-inch finishing nails can be driven through the subflooring and into the joist. Of course, this means that you will have to remove any tiles in the area. The tiles can either be partially pulled back or replaced, as discussed earlier.

You may be required to repair a sagging subfloor before you install your tile floor. When this condition is found, it is generally because the floor joists and girders have been weakend by rot or by insects. A weak and sagging floor first has to be raised to its proper level. If it is the first floor and there is a basement underneath it, the work can be done by a do-it-yourselfer. Use heavy lumber and a screw jack to accomplish the work.

The size of the lumber should be about 4 × 4 inches. Place one of the timbers on the basement floor directly under the sag and put the screw jack on top of it. This beam will distribute the weight of the floor over a relatively large portion of the basement floor. If the basement flooring is thick concrete, this step won't be necessary.

Next, nail a piece of 4 × 4 along the sagging joists. Use a third piece of timber as a vertical beam. Place it on the top of the jack so that it runs under the portion of the 4 × 4 that is nailed to the joists.

Don't attempt to bring the floor to a level position all at once. If this is done, you may crack the walls and ceilings in the rooms above. By raising the jack only a fraction each week, you will avoid doing extensive damage to the house.

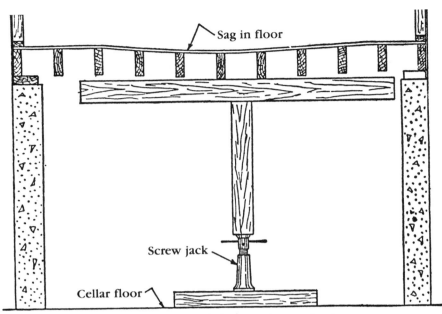

6-18 Installing a screw jack to repair a sagging floor.

Check the position of the floor with a level and, when it is correct, measure the distance from the bottom of the horizontal 4 × 4 to the floor of the basement. Cut a piece of 4 × 4 to this length. Turn the jack up enough to allow this beam to stand on end under the horizontal 4 × 4. Make sure that the beam is perfectly vertical and that is rests firmly on the floor. Remove the jack, along with the other timbers. Leave only one vertical and one horizontal 4 × 4.

If the entire floor sags, you will probably need to use more than one vertical support. In this case, place a vertical 4 × 4 under each end of the horizontal beam.

When part of the total weight of the floor and the objects on it is supported by posts, it is important that each post have the proper footing. Most concrete basement floors are rather thin. So, it is often necessary to prepare the floor before installing the posts.

To make a substantial footing for the posts that will rest on the basement floor, break up about 2 square feet of the concrete floor at the point where the post will stand. Do this work with a heavy hammer or with a piece of pipe. Once the surface is broken, dig a hole about 12 inches deep and fill it with concrete made with 1 part cement, 2 parts sand, and 3 parts coarse aggregate. Level this mixture with the floor and smooth the surface. Allow about a week for the footing to dry before you place the posts on it. Cover the concrete during this period and keep it moist.

Fortunately, most defects are associated with the first floor. The basement underneath it allows you to put in posts and other kinds of reinforcements. Sagging floors above the first floor level cannot practically be remedied, short of taking up the floor and making extensive repairs.

MAKING YOUR TILE FLOOR LAST

The best way to make repairs to resilient and hard-tile flooring is to prevent them. Careful preparation, a well-planned installation, and taking care of problems before they need to be repaired will help make your floor last. Follow the suggestions in Chapter 5 for floor maintenance for the type of floor covering installed in your home.

You can also reduce repairs dramatically by shopping wisely for quality flooring products rather than purchasing the lowest-priced items. Purchase your flooring where you can get valuable help and advice on the installation and care of your flooring. With the tile and money you are investing in your flooring, you want expert advice, not sales clerk guesses.

Another bit of advice offered by tile installers, which has helped many do-it-yourselfers, is to test first. Before you lay out your first floor, lay down a scrap piece of plywood and practice the installation. You can also begin where the refrigerator will be installed or within a closet where any goofs will not be as evident.

The same practice is good advice for the first time you strip a floor or use special flooring preparations. Find an area out of the way to test the product or technique before you use it on the main part of the floor. Doing so will possibly save the replacement or repair of a portion of the flooring.

Finally, don't be ashamed of calling an expert for advice if you have problems. Even if you didn't purchase the products at their store, most floor covering retailers will offer advice free of charge. They may not be familiar with the characteristics of the brands of tile and adhesive you purchased somewhere else, however. It's good value to get quality advice from the people who sell you a quality product. The extra few dollars you may spend will be good insurance.

Glossary

asphalt emulsion   A natural bituminous product, similar to tar, that is used as a waterproofing medium.

backing   Any material used as a base or crude framework, over which a finish material is to be applied. It is usually lumber, such as between studding to provide a more solid area over which metal lath can be nailed. Also refers to nail bearing boards used where studs or joists have been omitted.

beating in   The process of moving a small board over the tile while striking it lightly with a hammer, which sets the tile firmly into the mortar and creates a smooth, level plane.

bisque   The body of the tile, which is made of some type of clay, excluding the glaze. Sometimes called the biscuit.

bond   Refers to the adherence of one material to another, as of coats of mortar, tile to mortar, brick to mortar, etc. Also used to designate the patterns in which bricks are laid, as common bond, Flemish bond, etc., which indicates the arrangement or overlapping of bricks or stones that ties the wall together.

bush hammer   A hammer that has a rectangular head and two corrugated or toothed faces. It is used for roughing concrete to provide a masonry bond.

buttering   Coating the tile, also the mortar, with a mixture of pure cement and water to hold the tile in place and to make a bond between the tile and the mortar.

caulking   Refers to the filling in of joints or crevices with a type of mastic or by tamping in oakum or other wadding.

caulking compound   Originally a product made by saturating oakum with asphalt or tar; used for filling cracks, as in ships. Now the term refers to any putty-like compound that is waterproof and used for filling cracks around windows, etc. Many modern types are known as mastic.

cement   A product of certain types of limestone that contains lime, silica, and alumina, some kinds of which must be roasted and then pulverized. It hardens under water and is used in many types of mortar to bond sand together. When set, it is very hard.

ceramic   An article made of baked clay. In the tile trade, the word is used to designate a tile made of compressed clay and silica, which is rather glassy or vitreous in nature and will not absorb water.

chase   A type of construction that makes use of the rabbet principle. Glass blocks are commonly set into such a channel to lock them in place at the edges of panels.

chipping off   Cutting away mortar or concrete with a sharp-edged tool such as a hammer or chisel.

crystal   A rather rough, transparent glaze that has greater depth than ordinary glazes and imparts a design effect to the tile.

dutchman   A path made on a wood surface as a repair when too much wood has been taken away, or when an unnecessary cutout has been made.

efflorescence   A white powder, which is actually fine crystals of the soluble salts contained in mortar, that appears on concrete after it has set for a few days. Often referred to as alkali.

encaustic   Refers to the art of etching clay tiles and filling them in or inlaying them with another color of clay. After smoothing, the tiles are baked to harden them.

etched   Cut into the face or engraved.

expansion strips   Strips of cork or sometimes soft fiber sheets that are saturated with asphalt or other waterproofing. The strips are used at the edges of glass panels or concrete to provide room for expansion when the panels become warm.

fresno   A large, cement-finishing trowel that is fitted with a long wood handle, like a hoe, that pivots. It permits troweling of large areas without the need to walk on the concrete surface.

furring   Stripping used to build out a surface, such as a studded wall. Strips of suitable size are added to the studs to accommodate vent pipes or other fixtures.

gauging   The placement of strips at a desirable distance from the wall being tiled that act as a guide to maintain a required thickness of mortar.

glaze   Melted silica, or sand, that coats the tile body or bisque and gives it a transparent, glassy finish. It is somewhat harder than ordinary glass.

gloss   A bright or shiny finish that reflects light much like glass. Also the luster of a polished surface.

hydraulic   Denotes a force exerted by water, as the setting of cement through the action of water combining to form a catalyst.

lacquer A varnish-like product made from the resinous substance obtained from the lac insect of India. It is mixed with an ethyl alcohol.

lath A wood strip or metal mesh that receives the plaster and acts as a background or reinforcing agent for the plaster.

Masonite A trade name for a type of fiberboard that is made of cane fiber and pressed under great pressure to form a thin, hard sheet.

mastic A name applied to various sticky or sometimes putty-like substances, which are made of true resins with whiting and other materials added. It never hardens completely; its pliability makes it useful for many purposes, including the setting of tile.

matte A semirough glaze, that has a surface similar to an eggshell.

mold To form a pliable substance into some desired shape. It is generally done by pressing the material into a form or box provided for the purpose.

monolith Refers to a pillar or column of a single stone. When concrete is poured to form such a pillar, it is referred to as monolithic pouring, since it is all of one aggregate. This would not be true if concrete were poured over large stones.

mortar A combination of sand, cement, either fireclay or lime, and water, which is often used in the installation of hard tiles.

mosaic Small bits of tile, stone, glass, etc., that form a surface design of intricate pattern. It is often laid over mortar or metal.

mural A sort of picture done with small pieces of tile and intended for use on a wall as a decorative effect.

oakum Jute or hemp fibers loosely twisted together and saturated with asphalt or other tar-like material. It is used for caulking.

patio A Spanish word that means courtyard or inner court. It has come to be used in America to designate a partly enclosed porch; hence the tile used on such a floor is known as patio tile.

patty tile A corruption of the word patio, it refers to large clay tiles that are used for patio floors.

patty trowel A term used to describe a trowel intermediate in size between a pointer and a mason's trowel. It is used to pack damp mortar.

pier Usually a short built-up or cast column that is free standing; that is, not joined to other work and designed to support horizontal beams, such as floor stringers.

plastic A pliable substance capable of being molded or formed.

pointing Filling in joints with mortar or repairing holes. See tuck pointing.

quarry Used to designate tiles that are large and thick, similar to slabs of stone cut in a quarry. These are vitreous tiles and require no soaking.

refractories Clays or clay-like products that do not fuse or melt readily. They are suitable for tile bisques since they will not melt when the glaze is baked over the surface.

relief   Part of a design that projects beyond the plane or face of a molded or sculptured design.

riser   The upright portion of a stair step that supports the front of the tread. The part that keeps the toe from getting under the tread.

satin matte   A glaze intermediate between high gloss and common matte that imparts a silky sheen to the tile.

scarifier   A piece of thin sheet metal that has teeth or serrations cut in the edge like a saw blade. It is used to roughen mortar surfaces to provide a good bond. Also known as a scratcher.

screed   A strip of wood, often 2 × 4 inches, that is set down as a guide for attaining a level surface of concrete. In the tile trade, it refers to a piece of wood used as a straightedge.

silica   A natural quartz occurring as clear crystals or as sand with various other minerals in the mixture.

silicon   The chief ingredient of sand or glass, it is nonmetallic and, when melted, is more or less transparent and glassy. A form of quartz.

stretcher   A term used to designate the individual pieces of tile trim with the exception of in or out angles. The latter are always known by their regular names, such as in in angles, out angles, up angles, or down angles.

tapping in   The act of hitting tile lightly with the handle of the pointer as a preliminary means of setting them into place.

terra-cotta   A composition of clay and fine sand, either red or yellowish in color, used in making tile bisques, hollow tile, or flue linings.

terrazzo   A type of floor or wall finish obtained by embedding small-sized pebbles or crushed rock in concrete and grinding and polishing the surface to a smooth finish.

texture   The type of glaze or finish used in tiles. The texture may be high glass, matter, or somewhat etched.

tuck pointing   The process of filling in crevices, as with mortar, mastic, etc.

unglazed   Refers to pressed and baked tiles with a smooth, earthy surface, and no glaze.

vitreous   A substance that is glassy in texture and contains sand that has been melted. Vitreous tiles will not absorb water.

Index